Backyard Chickens

A Fifth-Generation Backyard Chicken Owner Shares His Family Secrets To Keeping A Happy, Productive & Healthy Flock

Geoff Evans

© COPYRIGHT 2020 By Geoff Evans
All Rights Reserved

The content contained within this book may not be reproduced, duplicated, or transmitted without direct written permission from the author or the publisher.

Under no circumstances will any blame or legal responsibility be held against the publisher, or author, for any damages, reparation, or monetary loss due to the information contained within this book. Either directly or indirectly. You are responsible for your own choices, actions, and results.

Legal Notice:

This book is copyright protected. This book is only for personal use. You cannot amend, distribute, sell, use, quote or paraphrase any part, or the content within this book, without the consent of the author or publisher.

Disclaimer Notice:

Please note the information contained within this document is for educational and entertainment purposes only. All effort has been executed to present accurate, up to date, and reliable, complete information. No warranties of any kind are declared or implied. Readers acknowledge that the author is not engaging in the rendering of legal, financial, medical, or professional advice. The content within this book has been derived from various sources. Please consult a licensed professional before attempting any techniques outlined in this book.

By reading this book, the reader agrees that under no circumstances is the author responsible for any losses, direct or indirect, which are incurred as a result of the use of the information contained within this document, including, but not limited to, — errors, omissions, or inaccuracies.

Your Free Gift (Egg Laying Tracker!)

As a thank you for downloading or purchasing this book, I'd love to give you my free Backyard Chicken Keeping Tracker – it allows you to easily and quickly track eggs laid, any chicken health issues that arise, cleaning, as well as any income and expenses associated with your new hobby!

To access it, simply go to

https://bit.ly/yourchickenkeepinglog

No email address required. Simply download the PDF, print & then it's all yours to use!

With that out of the way, let's get to the book!

Table of Contents

INTRODUCTION 7

CHAPTER 1 - IS KEEPING CHICKENS FOR YOU? 11

CHAPTER 2 - SELECTING YOUR BREEDS 29

CHAPTER 3 – DESIGNING YOUR FIRST COOP & RUN.. 47

CHAPTER 4 – BUYING & BRINGING CHICK(EN)S HOME! 69

CHAPTER 5 - FOOD, WATER & NUTRITION NEED-TO-KNOWS 84

CHAPTER 6 – THE STORY OF THE EGG & ALL ABOUT LAYING... 101

CHAPTER 7 – CHICKEN PSYCHOLOGY & THE PECKING ORDER.. 124

CHAPTER 8 – BEWARE THE GARDEN! (& THE PREDATORS).. 137

CHAPTER 9 – OPTIMAL CHICKEN HEALTH & SIMPLE TREATMENTS 155

CHAPTER 10 – CHICKEN KEEPING MYTHS DESTROYED 181

CHAPTER 11 – FLOCK MAINTENANCE & BUTCHERING BROILERS 189

CHAPTER 12 - MAKING MONEY & SHOWING OFF 213

CONCLUSION 231

COMMONLY ASKED QUESTIONS (& ANSWERS) 235

REFERENCES 247

Introduction

Maybe you've heard about backyard chickens in the media, or read a blog about the advantages of keeping chickens. Maybe your friends or neighbors keep chickens. Whatever prompted you to pick up this book, you're obviously curious about keeping backyard chickens, but you're not sure where to start. How do you choose your chickens? Will they fit in your backyard? How do you build a chicken coop? Actually, what is a chicken coop? And what on earth should you feed your chickens?

If those questions, or any others you might have, are holding you back - you're in the right place. In this book, I'll cover everything beginners (or even people with a bit of experience) need to know to get started raising backyard chickens, from beginning to end.

From the basics of time, space, and money, all the way to selling eggs and slaughtering chickens, I'll walk you step-by-step through what you need to know to succeed in your newfound hobby. You'll learn not only where to buy your chickens, how to choose a coop and how to protect your chickens against predators, but also about beginners' biggest misconceptions, chicken psychology, and how to identify and care for sick chickens. You'll even find out how to make some extra cash from your new venture, and maybe even show off your chickens at exhibitions!

My family has raised backyard chickens for more than four-generations before me. It's safe to say that we know a thing or two about the topic! Being around the farm so much as a child, I learned so much and always really enjoyed looking after our chickens. I promised myself that one day when I settled down, I'd get my own flock. I settled down about ten years ago, bought my first pullets a few months later, and haven't looked back since. So many people ask me about my chickens, wanting to know what's involved and how to get started, that I decided to write this book as a reference for people like you.

Keeping chickens is satisfying and rewarding on every level. There are tangible rewards of fresh eggs and fresh meat, and the environmental rewards of reducing food transport emissions. There's the satisfaction of raising your own food, the entertainment value of watching and caring for your flock, the benefits of chicken droppings in your compost heap, and the natural chemical-free pest control for your garden! If you have children, the responsibility they'll learn from looking after and interacting with chickens, and the educational advantages of becoming intimately familiar with the cycle of life and the food chain will stand them in good stead in all aspects of their lives.

By the time you finish this book, you'll be ready to set up your coop and get started. Unlike other books on Amazon, my book covers absolutely everything you need to know at each stage of your journey. It even covers what to grow in your garden (and what to avoid) so that you don't accidentally poison your chickens - and so much more.

What are you waiting for? Let's get you started on your backyard chicken journey!

Chapter 1 - Is Keeping Chickens For You?

You'll get so much out of keeping chickens, but it's not a decision to make lightly: like all animals, chickens need regular care and appropriate facilities. They're an ongoing commitment, not something to take on a whim. This chapter explains what you need to know before deciding to keep a flock of backyard chickens.

Like everything in life, there are pros and cons. In my family's experience, though, the pros have always outweighed the cons. By the end of this chapter, you'll have enough information to form your own opinion! The advantages are further split into the direct advantages to you, as well as the wider benefits to society. I don't need to say too much about the most obvious advantage: fresh eggs. Fresh eggs from happy hens are higher in omega-3, vitamins E, A, D, and beta carotene. They are also lower in fat and cholesterol. They're much healthier and more nutritious than eggs from factory farms. The fact that you're not contributing to the misery of the hens crammed together on factory farms is also a huge bonus, especially to those readers conscious about animal welfare.

Chicken droppings are high in nitrogen (N), phosphorous (P), and potassium (K) - ever heard of NPK? It's a common, powerful compost additive that refers to the chemical symbols of each element on the periodic table. Add the droppings to your compost heap, and in a few months, it'll be ready to fertilize your plants and garden. You could even bag and sell the droppings, or the compost. Society benefits because the droppings don't wash into the local rivers, and you benefit from increased yield in your gardening endeavors. That brings us to our next benefit.

Chickens will eat almost anything, including your kitchen scraps; which reduces household waste and cuts down your feeding expenses. If you let your chickens roam the garden, they're great at keeping garden pests under control too. They'll eat beetles, spiders, flies, worms, slugs, and many more undesirable pests, helping to keep your garden pest-free without using artificial chemicals.

If you have children around, chickens are a great way to teach them everything from empathy and responsibility, to applied science, life cycles, and the food chain. As another bonus, they're entertaining and personable (the chickens I mean - I don't know about your kids). Even if they're not supposed to be pets, it's surprising how often they *flap, scratch and peck* their way into that role.

On a societal level, keeping chickens helps the environment by keeping food local; it contributes to self-sufficiency and improves public health. Factory farms feed their chickens incredibly high doses of antibiotics to compensate for the cramped conditions. This contributes to the evolution of antibiotic-resistant bacteria. Regular antibiotics are completely unnecessary for well-cared-for backyard chickens. Some European Union studies have shown that salmonella is also less prevalent in free-range flocks.

Don't make the mistake of thinking that keeping chickens is all fun and games, though. There are some issues you should consider. As well as the initial costs, you'll have ongoing costs and extra work to contend with. Food, cleaning, medicine, and supplements are just a few to name. Can you afford it? Furthermore, your local laws might not allow you to keep chickens (especially roosters), and if you need to apply for a permit, there's usually a small fee. Unfortunately, we're not the only creatures that think eggs - and chickens - are tasty. Depending on where you live, you might find local predators and pests attracted to your garden. Dogs, cats, owls, foxes, and snakes are a few predators known to eat chickens and their eggs.

Once you get chickens, you'll learn that chicken droppings are unavoidable. Chickens poo everywhere. And scratch up your garden hunting for worms. And dig it up for dust baths. You'll find yourself dealing with an incredible amount of dust and chicken poop, so be mentally prepared in advance. In addition, planning will become an integral part of your life. Everything from holidays (who'll look after the flock?) to chicken menopause (what to do when the chickens stop laying?) need to be planned. Even if you're comfortable with these issues, most chickens lay eggs for about three years, but they can live for up to ten. What will you do when they stop laying? If you have children, are you comfortable explaining that decision to them?

I can't tell you whether backyard chickens are right for you, but I can give you the information to make that decision yourself. If you have time and money, and your current aims include staying healthy, creating a more sustainable world, teaching your children, and learning new things yourself, it's definitely a viable option.

A common concern when people have when considering keeping chickens is, "How much time will this take?" Fortunately, the answer is, "Not as much as you think." Unlike many pets, chickens are fairly self-sufficient. If you let them roam your garden, they'll keep themselves entertained.

You can find details of daily, weekly, and other tasks in Chapter 11, but in general, your daily tasks should take less than fifteen minutes a day. Once a week, you'll need about half an hour to clean the coop, and a few times a year, you'll need to deep-clean the coop. A deep clean still only takes a couple of hours, although it depends on the sort and the size of coop you have. Chicks require more attention as you'll need to keep a closer eye on them. However, if you keep the incubator in the house, it's not too much extra effort.

How much space you need depends on several factors, including the number and breed of chickens, the local climate, and how you plan to manage garden time. As a rule-of-thumb to get you going, **you'll need about three square feet per chicken in the coop**, ten inches of perching space per chicken on the roosting perches, and at least fifteen square feet for each chicken to roam. If you have individual nesting boxes rather than an open-plan layout, allow at least one cubic foot per hen. In almost every case, more room is better, with the exception of the coop. If the coop is too big, the chickens will get cold. When planning your coop layout, don't over-optimize; chickens also need enough space to fly onto and down from the roost without bumping into obstructions like feeders, waterers, and walls.

Contrary to what some people believe, chickens are personable and intelligent, with complex behaviors and social structures. People are very quick to judge. Pigs are often lauded for being extremely fat i.e., the common sayings "as fat as a pig", "I ate like a pig!" etc. However, I bet you didn't know that the average pig actually has a lower body fat percentage than the average human in America now! - [Mitchell, A. D et al. (1996)] Back to what I was saying, getting familiar with "normal" chicken behavior helps you to manage your flock. Unusual or uncharacteristic behaviors can give you early warning of developing problems.

Chickens are social birds and prefer to live with a flock. In the wild, they live in flocks of twelve to fifteen hens for every one rooster. They have a very strict pecking order, with a dominant rooster at the top, and the hens ranked below. The same hierarchical structure applies to backyard flocks. We'll discuss the pecking order in more detail later on.

When chickens sleep, they really sleep: they'll sleep soundly through rain, snow, and even predator attacks. To compensate, they prefer to sleep as far from the ground as possible, and in a shelter to protect them from overhead predators and the weather. This is helpful for you, as they won't need too much encouragement to come home to roost.

All chickens hate getting wet, but they love dust baths. They'll happily scratch out holes for dust baths in any exposed soil, lawn, garden, dust, or even litter. This helps them control parasites, and there's nothing you can do to stop it. If you give them a sandpit, they might use that instead of your vegetable garden, but there's no real guarantee.

Different countries and even different regions, have varying restrictions on keeping backyard chickens. I can't list every country below, so make sure you check your local laws if your country isn't included in the summary here. Neighbors' and officials' main objections to backyard chickens are noise (especially with roosters), and attracting vermin or predators. If your area does allow backyard chickens, get yourself a copy of the relevant regulations. First, it'll help you make sure you comply; and second, you might need to show it to your neighbors, if they're the difficult kind.

Australia

In general, chickens are generally allowed as long as you look after them properly. Your neighbors are more likely to be the cause of problems than the local council or the government. Because the specific laws vary by state and local council, you should contact your local Town Hall for information about "poultry keeping on a small scale."

Canada

If you live in a Canadian city, roosters aren't allowed due to noise laws, but some municipalities allow backyard hens. Apparently, most Canadian officials don't hunt for illegal backyard chickens, but they do respond to complaints. If you get on with your neighbors (or are willing to bribe them with eggs), you should be fine.

Europe

In the European Union (EU), most law relates to the import/export of animals, and large-scale farming. Each country has unique laws. In general, it's more acceptable to keep a backyard chicken flock in rural areas than in urban areas. Check your government's website, and ask at your local Town Hall.

The United Kingdom

According to the Department for the Environment, Food and Rural Affairs (DEFRA), it's fine to keep backyard chickens in the UK. Your local council, housing association, or landlord may disagree, so check with them first. Even if you own your home, check your house deed; some have a clause preventing or limiting the keeping of livestock (including chickens). Since the most recent bird flu outbreak, a flock of more than fifty poultry (including geese, turkeys, and chickens) is considered "commercial" and needs to be registered with DEFRA.

The United States of America

In the USA, keeping chickens depends completely on zoning regulations and your state, town, and community laws. If you live in an agricultural zone, you should be fine, but if you're in an urban or suburban area, double-check your local rules first.

Do you like going on holiday? Me too. Luckily, keeping chickens doesn't mean you have to stay home forever, as long as you plan ahead. If you're away from home regularly, you should check your chicken-sitting options before you make a final decision about keeping chickens. If you're only going away for a few days, you can probably get away with using automatic doors and feeders to care for your flock. It's still a good idea to ask someone to check in on them once a day. The checks should include equipment function, collecting eggs, and looking for any obvious health problems in the flock. If the equipment fails and no-one checks on your chickens, you could be charged with neglect under local animal welfare laws.

Chickens dislike change. If you can find a chicken-sitter to look after them at your home, it's better for the chickens than sending them to a boarding house, lending them to a friend, or taking them traveling with you. You could ask your family, friends, or neighbors, find other people nearby who keep chickens and arrange a tit-for-tats to cover each other's' holidays, or hire a pet-sitter.

No matter who's looking after your chickens, do what you can to make their life easy. Leave them written instructions and make sure:

1. their coop is clean;
2. there's enough food on-site; and
3. everything they'll need is easy to find.

As a rule-of-thumb, you'll need about half a cup of feed and two cups of water per chicken per day, plus a bit extra (just in case).

As a last resort, check for chicken boarding houses in your area. They're more common in some countries than others, but you won't know until you check. Before you leave your chickens anywhere, including at a chicken boarding house, visit it to check that the facilities are appropriate. In a well-run boarding house, the coops should be cleaned regularly and disinfected after each stay. The chickens should appear happy and healthy, and the building should be secure.

Backyard chickens are an investment. You'll need to consider the upfront costs (coop, equipment, and chickens) as well as ongoing costs (food, bedding, maintenance, and medical). The prices in this chapter are intended as a very rough guide in US dollars. Your local costs will vary, so double-check before you dive in.

A simple coop is about $500, although you could easily spend over $2000 if you wanted. On the flip side, if you're good with tools, you can save some money by building your own. Alternatively, you could also cut costs by purchasing a second-hand coop. You'll find all kinds of tutorials and coop design ideas online. Depending on age, breed, and sex, chickens cost between $2 (for day-old chicks of common breeds) and $50 (for point-of-lay heritage breeds). About $20-$30 each is fairly typical. You can read more about this in Chapters 2 (Breed Selection) and 4 (Planning for and Buying Chickens). If you decide to buy chicks, you'll need to invest in a brooder ($75-$100, or build your own), and a heater. ($20-$30)

Your ongoing costs are food (typically less than $40 a month), bedding ($5-$15 a month), medicines and supplements (usually less than $10 a month), grit and scratch (about $5 every few months), treats, and pest control (budget around $10 a month, although it will likely be less). Visits to the vet, coop maintenance and repair, are occasional costs. The price of a visit to the vet varies wildly, depending on your vet and the problem. I can't give a meaningful estimate for coop maintenance. It depends on your coop, the condition it's in, whether you can do the work yourself, and whether you already have tools or spare parts around the house.

Should you raise turkeys alongside chickens?

The main argument against keeping chickens and turkeys together is that turkeys are susceptible to a disease called blackhead, which is carried by chickens. It can have serious consequences for turkeys and is very difficult to treat. That said, you can minimize the risk by worming regularly and by using isolation and quarantines for new chickens before introducing them to the turkeys. Plenty of people successfully raise turkeys and chickens together.

Blackhead isn't the only problem with keeping chickens and turkeys together. Unfortunately, chickens find turkey tails attractive and can follow them around, plucking the feathers. You can't really blame the turkeys for retaliating. Given the size difference, the end result can be messy!

On the other hand, keeping turkey poults (i.e., turkey hatchlings) with chicks can help the poults learn to eat and drink more quickly by mimicking the chicks. The chicks, in turn, acquire immunity to Marek's disease. Marek's disease is a virus that causes tumors in chickens. As an added bonus, if any of your hens are broody, you can keep them happy by giving them turkey eggs to hatch. Most broody hens will even look after a few extra poults if you slip them in with poults she's hatched.

How long do chickens live?

Matilda famously holds the Guinness World Record for the longest-living hen. She lived for sixteen years! Most hens don't live that long, but if you look after them properly, most hens will lay eggs for around three years and can live for up to ten years. The keys to a long life for your hens are good housing, quality food, good care, and the freedom to behave as they want! Personality and breed also play a part. Some chickens are naturally smarter than others, and will naturally watch out for predators and stick closer to shelter, which improves their survival rate. Likewise, some breeds naturally live longer than others. If you take good care of your chickens, keep their coop clean, feed them, water them and treat them well, they'll be with you for a long, long time.

In the next chapter, you'll get to figure out which breeds of chicken are best for you (and see pictures of some beautiful and rare birds).

Chapter 2 - Selecting Your Breeds

It should come as no surprise to you that different breeds have different characteristics. Before choosing your chickens, you need to decide your primary goals: eggs, meat, a lovable pet, a bird you can take to shows and competitions, or some combination of these?

Chicken breeds can be divided into several categories. The first thing you should know is that each breed is either a heritage breed or a hybrid. Heritage breeds are the "purebreds" of the chicken world. They grow more slowly than hybrids, which means they keep laying eggs for longer. They can live for up to eight years, whereas hybrids live from three to six years. Hybrids start laying sooner than heritage breeds, but they slow down sooner as well. They often stop laying by the time they're two, and they're generally prone to more diseases.

Another way of categorizing chickens is as egg-producing breeds, meat-producing breeds (broilers), or dual-purpose breeds. These categories are fairly self-explanatory.

The five most popular egg-producing breeds are as follows:

Rhode Island Red - Rhode Island reds are a heritage breed developed in the USA. They lay up to 260 eggs a year and grow to  seven pounds, making them a popular dual-purpose chicken too. They start laying when they're between eighteen and twenty-four weeks old and are an attractive, friendly, easy-going breed that thrive in cold temperatures. They're also good foragers.

Leghorn - The Leghorn breed comes from Livorno, Italy. They come in twelve different colors, but the white chickens lay the most eggs (up to 280 a year). Bred to handle hot climates,  leghorns grow to about six pounds, and start laying when they're between sixteen and twenty-one weeks old. They are fantastic foragers, highly fertile, and hardy. The eggs they lay are typically white in color.

Golden Comet – The Golden Comet is a hybrid breed, bred for high egg production. Golden Comet hens lay up to 300 eggs a year and grow to seven pounds. They're very calm chickens that get on well with other animals. Unfortunately, like many hybrids, they're prone to tumors and other health problems, so they often die before they're five years old.

Plymouth Rock - Plymouth Rocks can grow to seven pounds. They're very

popular as both egg-producing and dual-purpose chickens, and start laying between eighteen and twenty-two weeks. They're tame, very friendly chickens that get on well with children and other birds. As a bonus, they're fantastic foragers, and they handle harsh elements well.

Americaunas - also known as Easter egg chickens, they too are a hybrid breed. They only lay about 180 to 250 eggs a year, but their multicolored eggs are very popular for both their colors and their low cholesterol levels. Americaunas are small

birds, only growing to about five pounds, and they start laying eggs at between 25 and 30 weeks. They can live up to eight years. The down-side is that they're prone to a genetic disorder called "crossed beak."

Meat-producing breeds (broilers) grow faster than egg-producing breeds, so they experience health problems such as broken legs and heart issues if they're not slaughtered once fully grown. **Meat chickens** are usually more docile and a little lazier.

The most popular meat-producing breeds *(broilers)* for backyard flocks are:

Cornish Cross - Cornish Cross chickens are a popular meat-producing breed for both commercial and backyard flocks. The roosters can grow to twelve pounds in only six to eight weeks, while the females grow to about eight pounds. Unsurprisingly, they're not very active chickens, not least because they spend so much energy digesting all the food they eat. They're difficult to breed in an incubator, so you'll need to buy them as chicks.

Jersey Giant - Jersey Giants were intended to replace turkeys when they were developed in the USA. Even though this didn't happen, they're still very large birds. They take sixteen to twenty-one weeks to grow to their full size of around twelve pounds. Because of their slow growth rate, if you don't grow your own feed, feeding your Jersey Giants can be expensive. The hens are docile, and are actually reasonable layers, while the roosters are occasionally aggressive. They're easy to breed and aren't as prone to health issues as the Cornish Cross, making them popular for backyard flocks.

La Bresse - La Bresse is a traditional French breed that's widely considered the best-tasting meat chicken in the world. As a bonus, it's also a pretty good layer. La Bresse chickens grow to six or seven pounds in sixteen to twenty weeks, and the hens lay up to 180 eggs a year. They're expensive to buy, but once you have a breeding pair, they're peaceful, docile, and surprisingly easy to breed.

Delaware - As the name suggests, Delaware chickens originate from the USA. They're a cross between the Plymouth Rock and New Hampshire Red and are popular as both a meat-producing and a dual-purpose breed. They can grow to nine pounds in only twelve weeks.

Freedom Ranger - Freedom Rangers are a great choice of meat bird, and are fantastic foragers. If you give them enough space to forage properly, they'll thrive on bugs and corn. This makes them a perfect choice as a free-range chicken, but they do take some time to grow. You can harvest them at five or six pounds, which is usually around at around ten weeks old.

Regardless of which meat-producing breed you choose, you'll need to fatten them correctly. One of the problems of meat-producing breeds is that, in general, they're lazy. Since the best meat is muscle, not fat, you need to encourage your birds to exercise. A simple yet effective way to do this is to put the water on the opposite side of the pen from the food. This forces them to move around somewhat more.

There are several schools of thought for the best way to feed chickens for maximum growth. Some insist that food should always be available, while others argue that chickens don't eat in the dark and advocate for a 12 on/12 off schedule. That means giving them unlimited access to food for twelve hours, then removing it when it's dark. There's even a group who argue for leaving the lights on 24/7, to encourage them to eat at night, but I wouldn't recommend that, personally. I prefer to give them access to food at all times. It's less trouble, and leaving the lights on at all hours doesn't do much good for the environment either. The only concern with having food constantly available is that exposed food can attract pests, so you'll need to be diligent about keeping the area around the feeders clean, and not overfeeding. We'll talk more about feeding later on in the book.

Dual-purpose breeds aim to give you the best of both worlds: consistent egg production, and lots of meat. (when you do eventually slaughter the chickens) The main down-side of dual-purpose chickens is that you (and your children) have more time to get attached to them. This can make it difficult when slaughter-day arrives.

I've covered the Rhode Island Red, Plymouth Rock, and Delaware breeds as either egg or meat-producing breeds, but the aforementioned breeds are also very popular dual-purpose chickens. **As well as these, other popular dual-purpose chicken breeds are:**

Australorps – My favorite breed, and the one that made me fall in love with keeping chickens! Australorps were first bred in Australia by the Austral Orpington Club. They're beautiful, friendly chickens and they make great mothers. They lay around 260 eggs a year (although once, one managed 364 eggs in 365 days!), and they grow to about seven or eight pounds. Australorps start laying at about twenty-two weeks, they're resistant to cold and are happiest in an open space. Their only significant drawback is that they don't get on well with other breeds: they bully them, and will sometimes even eat their eggs.

Orpington - Orpingtons are a heritage breed, often used as exhibition birds. They grow slowly and can live for over eight years. They have stunning colors, lay around 150 eggs a year, and grow to about six or seven pounds. They're resistant to cold, very friendly to humans, and great at foraging. One issue to consider is that their fluffy coats retain moisture, so they need a good shelter. They also don't fly well, so they can't escape predators. Orpingtons are the base breed for several other well-known breeds, including Australorps.

Wyandotte - As well as being popular exhibition birds because of their beautiful feather patterns,

Wyandottes lay more than 200 eggs a year and grow to six or seven pounds. They're quite hardy, can handle heat and cold, and are quite broody. If you're planning to breed chickens, a few Wyandottes will make your new hobby a breeze.

[Golden Laced Wyandotte – Left & Silver Laced Wyandotte - Right]

Sussex - Sussex chickens are calm, curious, friendly, good-looking birds. The hens start laying between sixteen and twenty weeks of age, and lay up to 250 eggs each year. Both sussex hens and roosters grow to at least seven pounds. Sussex chickens don't need much

space, but it's not a good idea to keep them in a mixed flock: they're easily bullied by other birds.

The first thing you'll notice about **bantam breeds** is that they're smaller: on average, they're about a quarter or a fifth the size of standard breeds. When sailors first saw the tiny chickens in Bantam, Indonesia, that was the first thing they noticed as well, but it's not the only difference. As you'd expect, Bantam chickens lay smaller eggs; but what you may not expect is that their eggs have less white and more yolk than standard chicken eggs. Most bantams start laying steadily from about eight months of age.

There are three categories of bantam breeds:

1. True bantams
2. Miniaturized bantams, and
3. Developed bantams

True bantams occur naturally, while miniaturized and developed bantams have been artificially bred. Bantams normally live about seven or eight years, but can live for up to twelve. There are numerous bantam breeds, and their needs aren't significantly different from standard breeds. Because they're smaller, they're more sensitive to cold, and they need less space than larger chickens - about two square feet per chicken in the coop and four in the run should be enough.

In a mixed flock, they're often targets for larger bullies. Fortunately, they're good flyers, so they have a chance to escape! Many bantams are "sablepoots," which means they have feathered legs. These feathers need to be kept clean and checked at least monthly for mites. To help keep leg feathers clean, add pebbles, mulch, or sand and try to minimize mud in the area. Keep styptic powder handy to control bleeding from broken leg feathers, and if they get too dirt-encrusted, stand the bird in warm water and clean them gently.

In general, bantams are friendly and curious, with a sweet temperament. They're attractive, and popular as both show birds and pets. If you don't have much space, you should strongly consider bantam breeds.

See & Taste the rainbow!

Most people probably picture chicken eggs as either white or tan. But not you! Different breeds lay eggs in colors ranging from chocolate brown to green, to pink and blue. While egg color doesn't affect nutrition, seeing a rainbow of egg colors brings delight to children and adults alike!

If you want **blue eggs**, add some Araucanas (including Ameraucanas) or Cream Legbars to your flock. For **chocolate brown eggs**, you'll want Marans, Welsummers, Barnevelders, or Penedesencas. **Green eggs**, ranging from olive to mint green, are the domain of Olive Eggers (half-Marans, half-Ameraucana), Favaucanas (half-Faverolle, half-Ameraucana) and Isbars. Eggs ranging from **cream to pale pink** come from Light Sussex, Mottled Javas, Australorps, Buff Orpingtons, Silkies, and Faverolles. In contrast to the all the rainbow colors, Leghorns, Andalusians, Anconas, Lakenvelders, Polish, and Hamburg hens will give you **pure white** eggs.

All chicken feathers (also known as plumage) would be white without pigmentation. In most environments, white birds would be highly visible and be a prime target for predators. Evolutionary pressure led to the colors we see today. Technically speaking, chicken plumage only has two pigments: red and black. The red pigment creates the range of feather colors we see today, ranging from light lemon to deep mahogany. In many cases, the name of the breed tells you the main color (e.g., Buff Orpington, Rhode Island Red, Gold-Laced Wyandotte), while cross-breeding makes for some stunning color combinations. We'll talk about choosing a show breed as part of Chapter 12.

As with all animals, some chicken breeds are better at coping with cold climates. These chickens usually have small combs, large bodies, and heavy feathering. They often have feathered feet as well. These chickens fair well, even in sub-zero temperatures.

Of the breeds we've already discussed, several are well-adapted to the cold:

- Rhode Island Red;
- Leghorn;
- Ameraucana;
- Orpington;
- Australorp;
- Wyandotte;
- Sussex; and

- Brahma.

As a general rule, hens are less susceptible to cold than roosters, mainly because of their smaller combs. If you're concerned your birds may get too cold, consider a well-secured heat source. An infrared light bulb works well as long as it's out of easy reach of your birds and placed somewhere which isn't a fire risk to your coop. A little bit of vaseline on your chickens' combs helps to prevent frostbite, and a heated waterer combats their water from freezing.

Chapter 3 – Designing Your First Coop & Run

After selecting your breed(s), housing is the next most important consideration. Before your chickens arrive, you'll need a coop, a run, a roost, a nesting area, and fencing. Of those, the coop is the biggest investment, so let's begin there.

A chicken coop, sometimes called a henhouse, is the shelter where your chickens spend their nights and sometimes take shelter from the weather. It contains an indoor roost and nesting area, and a fenced-in outdoor area. Coops come in a range of designs and materials. Regardless of which design or material you choose, there are four general principles you should bear in mind:

- First, your coop needs to be well-ventilated and big enough for the number

of chickens you intend to keep. If your coop is too small or poorly ventilated, your birds will be prone to respiratory diseases, aggression, and other stress-related behavioral problems;
- Second, your coop should keep your chickens cool in summer, but warm in winter, and safe from predators. This means you should have adequate insulation, and some way to securely lock the door;
- Third, you need to be able to easily access the coop to facilitate cleaning and egg collection; and
- Fourth, storage, power, and water need to be readily available.

As I mentioned in Chapter 1, if you have an outside run and standard-size chickens, you'll need about 3 square foot per chicken in the coop, about 10 inches of perching space per chicken in the roost, and at least 1 cubic foot per hen if you use individual nesting boxes.

If you're keeping bantams, you can get away with 2 square feet per chicken in the coop, while larger breeds will need at least 4 square feet per chicken. If there's no outside run, you'll need to allow 5-10 square feet per chicken, depending on your chickens' size. If you have space, a larger coop is better for ventilation and access, but if it's too large, your chickens may get cold. If you're not sure, err on the large side: you'll probably end up with extra chickens or chicks at some point anyway!

For ventilation, try to put several vents on each side of the coop that you can open and close as and when required. This helps to prevent moisture, ammonia (from the droppings), dust, and heat from building up. As a rule of thumb, if you're in a temperate area, aim for 1 square foot of vent per 10 square foot of coop space. In hot areas, increase that to 1.5 square feet per 10 square feet.

In cold areas, keep the vents above the level of the roost and protected from rain and snow; in warm areas, you can keep them lower down. It's better to have more vents than you think you'll need; as at worst, you can leave them closed. To ensure predators aren't a problem, make sure all openings (including vents) are covered at night, either by a door or by strong, fine mesh. If you have burrowing predators in your area, consider an elevated coop or deeply dug fencing. See Chapter 8 for more detail about preventing predator attacks!

Before you get too far with the layout, you need to consider your rooster - or roosters. If you want to breed your chickens, you'll obviously need at least one rooster. Some people worry about keeping roosters with their hens, but if you only have one rooster, it's not a problem. It actually tends to keep the hens happy. The problems in the pecking order start if you have more than one rooster in a flock. If you want multiple roosters, you'll need to ensure each rooster has enough hens (ten to twelve hens per rooster seems to work well) and lots of space. Problems begin when roosters are crowded together or are competing for too few hens. The exception is if you raise the roosters together, or introduce new roosters while they're still chicks (more about that later on).

At some point, you'll need to quarantine sick chickens or newly purchased chickens, isolate a bully, or keep some chickens separate for some other reason. If you have space when you're designing your coop and run, plan out a small isolation pen. It doesn't need to be too big. Three feet by six feet is enough to isolate one or two chickens from the rest of the flock. The isolation pen should have a separate drinker or feeder and should be self-contained.

Flooring
Your three options for flooring are dirt, concrete, or wood. Dirt floors are cheap but tend to be difficult to keep clean. Concrete floors are easy to clean, but expensive; while wooden floors are a good compromise. The problem with wooden floors is that they're prone to rotting if the coop isn't elevated, and they're difficult to

clean because the droppings get stuck between the planks. Varnishing the wood with a durable, non-toxic floor varnish can make it easier to clean, but it still isn't a perfect solution.

The roost might seem fairly straightforward, but it's still worth thinking about. Chickens' feet are flat when they sleep, so their roosting perch should be flat and between two and four inches wide. If you have bantams, you can get away with one inch. Remember, your chickens will spend up to twelve hours a night on their roosting perch, so make sure it's smooth and comfortable for them. If you're making your own, an untreated length of two by four inch wood, wide-side up, makes a perfect roosting perch. Please don't use plastic or metal.

Roosting perches should be 1.5 to 3 feet high, depending on your chickens. Small chickens tend to prefer a high roosting perch, while older and heavier chickens prefer to stay closer to the ground. If the perch is too high for your chickens, they're at risk of leg injuries when they jump down from high perches. When positioning your waterers, feeders, and nesting boxes, don't put them under the roost, or they'll get covered with droppings, again creating more work.

Speaking of nesting boxes, most chickens like to lay eggs in dark, protected places. If your nesting boxes don't fit these criteria, you may find yourself hunting all over the coop for eggs. Nesting boxes should be about 1 cubic foot for standard chickens, or 14" cubed for large chickens. You should provide one nesting box for every three or four hens. More than that, and your hens may become broody (inclined to incubate), and they may start laying somewhere else. In terms of design, a small lip on the boxes helps to keep the bedding from falling out, and a hinged lid will help you collect the eggs. To discourage your hens from laying eggs outside nesting boxes, try to minimize other dark, enclosed, or shadowy areas in the coop that hens might consider as cozy places to lay eggs.

Your coop also needs to fit in your available space. If you're lucky enough to have a choice about where to put it, there are a few things worth considering, mainly for your own convenience. Even though some local rules mandate a minimum distance between animal shelters and human habitations, it is easier to do daily chores like collecting eggs and refilling waterers if the coop is nearer to your house. You'll also have easy access to power for things like lights, heating, and power tools as and when you need them.

Don't forget to consider the weather. Can you position the coop to take advantage of breezes and shade in a hot climate, or provide extra shelter and a windbreak if in a cold climate? Will the prevailing wind blow odors from your coop to your house - or to your neighbors house? Do you have access to storage for feed, grit, and bedding near the coop? Planning and working out these details in advance takes time and effort, but not nearly as much time and effort as rebuilding or moving the coop after your chickens have moved in.

Buy or DIY? It's an ongoing debate, and both sides have some excellent points. Cost is the most obvious disadvantage of buying a chicken coop. It's more expensive, but it's also far less work; however, if you have the right skills, DIY offers the ultimate in flexibility and customization and results in you having a coop that is generally easier to maintain.

To make DIY simpler, you can convert an existing structure such as a dog kennel, or make one from scratch out of new or recycled materials. There are endless designs and how-to videos online. Whichever design you choose, make sure it meets the requirements which we already discussed, and double-check that you've removed all sharp edges (nails sticking out of old boards, or raw ends of wire) before your chickens arrive.

At a practical level, whether you buy it or build it, you'll want to be able to clean and maintain your coop without struggle. Having easy access turns this from a painful chore to a short, easy job. For cleaning, your most common job will be cleaning under the roost. If you fit a removable tray/dropping board under the roost, it will make this job considerably easier.

Once you have your coop built or bought, next on your all-important to-do list are bedding and floor litter. You can get away with anything safe for bedding, but floor litter should be dust-free and absorbent.

There are four popular types of chicken bedding and floor litter:

Straw - Straw is cheap, but you need to change it frequently. As a side note, make sure you get straw and not hay - hay is damp, contains seeds, and gets moldy easily.

Wood shavings - Wood shavings are cheap, absorbent, and smells fresh. The only catch is that you need to buy dust-extracted soft-wood shavings, and avoid cedar shavings, or your chickens will become more prone to respiratory issues.

Chopped cardboard - Like wood shavings, chopped cardboard is cheap, absorbent, and easy to clean out. Dust isn't a concern, and chopped cardboard has always been my favorite option.

Chopped hemp - Chopped hemp is a newcomer to the chicken bedding space. It's dust-free, absorbent, and composts easily. As a bonus, it repels flies.

Once you've got a grip on your coop, the run is next. A chicken run is the secure outdoor area for your chickens to roam, forage, take dust baths, and generally just act like chickens. In the run, unlike in the coop, more space is always better, so make it as big as you reasonably can. Fifteen square feet per chicken is the bare minimum.

Chickens aren't the best fliers, but most of them can manage to get a few feet off the ground. Bantams can even get up trees! If the fence around your chicken run is too low, you'll find your chickens escaping, or trying to! One option is to have a small, completely enclosed run attached to the coop. When you're not around, the chickens can safely use that. They'll be safe from predators, and your chickens won't be able to fly over the fence. When you're around to supervise, you can let them roam in a bigger space.

Fencing has two main functions: to keep your chickens in and to keep the predators out. Fencing also needs to be durable, easy to maintain, and compatible with your chicken coop. Keeping your chickens in is the easy part: a secure six-foot fence attached to the ground at the bottom will generally suffice. Protection from predators is more complicated. As well as being strong enough to keep predators out, fences need to extend at least six inches underground to protect against burrowing predators (like rats, raccoons, and weasels), and overhead, to protect against from other birds.

Broadly speaking, fencing options are split into standard fences and electric fences. The most common fencing options for raising chickens are chicken wire, hardware cloth, chain-link fence, and aviary netting. Some plastic fencing options exist, but they don't work well in my opinion.

Chicken wire seems like the obvious choice. It's cheap, and as the name suggests, it works well for keeping chickens in. Unfortunately, it's almost useless for keeping any but the smallest predators out. Hardware cloth is the next step up from chicken wire. It's more expensive, but it's a lot stronger, so it works well to keep most of the larger predators out. If large predators like bears are a problem in your area, hardware cloth won't work – you'd need a chain-link fence.

Fences obviously won't stop flying predators such as hawks and eagles, which is where aviary netting comes in really useful. Electric fencing is a simple solution to the problems that come with more traditional fencing materials. It's affordable and reliable, and works both for keeping chickens in (assuming it's high enough) and keeping ground predators out. Simple electric poultry fences plug into your home power supply, while more expensive systems operate from solar power and rechargeable batteries. Whichever electric fencing option you choose, if you have aerial predators in your area, you'll still need aviary netting. Use sturdy and well-anchored fence posts, bury the fencing material at least six inches, check the fence regularly, and you should be just fine.

Free-range

Free-ranging doesn't mean leaving your chickens outside to fend for themselves. It most cases, it means giving your chickens access to an area outside of their coop and pen. As the name suggests, this is likely to be your garden or yard!

Before you let your chickens out to free-range, take some time to think through and minimize the risks. Consider whether your chickens can get over your garden fence, whether predators can get in, and how closely you can supervise them while they're out.

Free-ranging is fantastic for chickens. They can supplement their diet by foraging, they get some exercise, and they have fun just doing normal chicken things. Free-ranging also has benefits for you. It lets your chickens eat up your garden pests, saves you money on feed, aerates and fertilizes your garden, increases hygiene, and provides more nutritious eggs and meat, with very little extra effort from you!

The main downside of letting chickens free-range is the mess. You'll find droppings everywhere, and they'll dig holes in your yard for dust baths, kick your mulch around, and make a meal of any unprotected vegetable patches. Free-range chickens are more exposed to predators, and sometimes hens will lay eggs in strange places that you might not see. Keeping a rooster with the flock can help to address safety issues. They usually protect the hens and will sound the alarm when predators are around.

Once you've settled on a coop and a run and you've decided what sort of bedding and fencing to use, it's time to start thinking about some additional equipment. If you're starting with eggs, you'll need an incubator, a humidity sensor, a thermometer, and a small bright flashlight for egg candling. While you could build an incubator, it's much easier to buy one, and they're not overly expensive.

If instead you're starting with chicks, you'll need sufficient gear to look after them until they're ready to move into the main coop. The first thing is the brooder. A brooder is a small enclosure or container to keep them in. It can be something from a simple box to a highly-optimized custom brooding house. As long as it can keep the chicks secure, protected, and draft-free, it'll do the job. As with full-grown chickens, chicks need bedding in the brooder. Again, avoid cedar shavings as they can cause respiratory problems. Some people use newspaper, but this isn't ideal for chicks as it's slippery and can lead to spraddled legs - an avoidable leg deformity.

To keep your chicks warm in the brooder, you'll need a heat lamp - 250 watts works best. A neat trick to deter chicks from pecking each other, is to use a red lamp (more about this in Chapter 8). As they grow, you'll need a separation pen to introduce them gradually to your main flock. You'll need appropriate feeders and waterers for all of your chickens, regardless of their age, size, or type. These can be as simple as a sturdy, stable bowl, or as complicated as automatic electronic systems. The main factors to think about are size and access. For chicks, make sure you choose a waterer that they can't fall into; as even if they don't drown, they can get too cold and die. Putting large, clean pebbles into the waterer can help with this. As with adult chickens, you'll need to provide grit to help them digest their food;

but note that chick grit is finer than grit for full-grown chickens.

When your chickens are fully-grown, a ten-pound plastic feeder will feed a flock of twenty-four hens for a day or two. Wall-mounted feeders take up less space, but hanging feeders allow better access, and chickens seem to enjoy them. Regardless of where you put your feeder, make sure it's protected from rodents and the weather, and ensure that it is not in the poop-zone under the roost.

There are all sorts of waterers on the market. Bowls are the simplest, but they're easy to contaminate; other systems are designed to prevent fouling and improve access. If you keep your waterer inside the coop, spillage will make the coop damp, which can lead to frostbite. If you live somewhere cold, water and coop heaters are worthwhile investments. If you like to sleep-in or you want the flexibility to come home late, an automatic door is worth considering. The downside is that slow chickens could be stuck outside, or predators might even get locked in with the chickens!

If you're raising laying hens (which is likely), another optional extra is a coop light on a timer to encourage your hens to keep laying in winter. Also, ensure you have a supply of empty egg cartons, egg-cleaning supplies, and a pen or wax pencil to mark the date you collected each egg.

If you're keeping chickens for meat, you'll find it useful to have equipment on hand for slaughter day. Practical equipment includes a killing funnel/cone; a waste bucket (or several!); a sharp knife, a sharpening stone and steel; a table (or plastic tablecloth); a pot large enough to hold a whole chicken; a gas burner, and a large cooler.

There are lots of supplies on the market to help you keep your chickens healthy. Which ones you keep in stock and which ones you buy as-needed is up to you.

Common items that I find useful to have around are Vaseline for frostbite, mites, and cracked heels, as well as styptic powder or spray to control bleeding from any broken feathers or wounds. Many people keep a stock of food-grade diatomaceous earth to prevent and treat mites and other parasites. If you use this, make sure you have a supply of dust masks, as it's not healthy to inhale.

That brings us onto the last category: personal protective equipment, or PPE. Dust masks protect you from inhaling dried droppings when you're cleaning your coop, gloves help protect you from chicken droppings and scratches, and a dedicated pair of durable rubber boots will prevent cross-contamination. Storage needs to be convenient, secure, watertight, and rodent-proof, particularly for feed. Feed needs to be stored in a cool, dry place to keep it in good condition. Metal dustbins are an inexpensive way to store feed and bedding, and you can put them almost anywhere.

Don't have much space?

Even if you really don't have much space, you still have some options if you want to keep chickens. If you have a small garden, you can reduce your coop's footprint with a multi-story coop. This is a raised coop with a run underneath it. It offers the same space as a standard coop and run, but it's a more efficient use of space. As a bonus for you, the coop is at waist height, which makes cleaning easier!

If you don't have enough space for a multi-story coop, some people keep one or two chickens as house pets. This requires planning and a lot of cleaning. I hear that an old chest of drawers can make a good base for a DIY indoor coop. If you choose to go down this route, a few minutes looking up information on chicken diapers will be an efficient use of your time!

Chapter 4 – Buying & Bringing Chick(en)s Home!

This chapter gets into the nuts and bolts of one of the most fun stages: actually buying your chickens. So, you know what breed you want, and how many, but should you buy eggs, chicks, pullets, point-of-lay, or adult chickens? It's is a matter of weighing up the price, work required, and convenience.

On the face of it, starting with eggs seems like a good plan. Fertilized eggs are cheaper than live chicks or chickens. However, there are two main disadvantages—first, the extra work. You'll need to hatch, raise, and feed the chicks for at least three or four months before you can start collecting eggs. Secondly, on average, about half of fertilized eggs hatch, and (again, on average) about half of those will be male. If you want six hens, on average, you'll need to hatch twelve eggs, which means you'll need to start with at least twenty-four eggs. Because these numbers are averages, it means that sometimes no eggs will hatch or sometimes all of them will hatch. Sometimes all the chicks will be male. You won't know for sure until one day you wake up with a flock of twenty-four roosters, or maybe one day none of your eggs hatch at all!

Day-old chicks are cheap to purchase, but as with the eggs, you'll have to feed them and raise them for at least three or four months before reaping the rewards. Pullets are normally about six to ten weeks old, but some people consider chickens to be pullets right up to twenty weeks. Pullets are fully feathered, but not yet fully grown. In price, pullets fall between that of chicks and point-of-lay chickens. They're big enough to move straight to an outdoor coop, but still young enough to tame. The main advantage of pullets is that they take less looking after than chicks.

This term is self-explanatory. Point-of-lay hens are hens that are ready to start laying.

They're usually about sixteen to twenty-two weeks old. The obvious benefit here is that you won't have to wait long for your eggs. Unsurprisingly, these are slightly more expensive than pullets, but only by a few dollars. If you want adult hens or layers, you'll usually have to buy them privately as hatcheries don't normally sell them. If you can find layers for sale, they'll be a few dollars more than a point-of-lay hen. Apart from not having to wait for eggs, the other advantage is that the seller might be able to tell you how many eggs those hens have been laying each week.

Once you know the age and breed you want to buy, you need to find out where to buy them. This depends entirely on what's available in your area. While you can transport chickens long distances, they don't like it, so you should avoid it if you can.

You can reliably find eggs, chicks, and chickens for sale in several places. Most places that sell chicks also sell fertilized eggs. Buying from a breeder is more expensive than other options, but it's a great choice if you have a breeder nearby. They're often passionate about their birds, so the birds you buy will be healthy and good quality. As a bonus, the breeder will be a great contact for information about what to expect and how best to look after your chickens, aside from myself and this book. You can find breeders through breed clubs and ads on poultry forums.

If you can get to a local poultry show, most poultry shows have sale pens where you can choose and buy birds. These are great places to look for a range of breeds and get advice from experienced chicken keepers. Alternatively, it's possible to buy birds at poultry auctions, but take extra care: some people use auctions to get rid of low quality or unhealthy birds. As always, caveat emptor - buyer beware.

Hatcheries are an easy, popular way to buy eggs, chicks, and chickens. You can order your chickens online from hatchery websites, and they'll deliver them to your door. If you can, try to order from your closest hatchery - chickens don't like traveling. As well as convenience, hatcheries often have a good range of breeds to choose from, and you can order vaccinated chickens. Apart from transport stressing your chickens, hatcheries often have high shipping costs (for obvious reasons) and high minimum orders for chicks, particularly in winter. This is to keep the chicks warm in transit and help them survive the journey. There's also an ethical problem: most hatcheries cull their roosters, but if this isn't a problem for you, hatcheries are a great choice.

Farm supply stores often sell chicks and pullets in spring. It's convenient, as you can get your birds and your supplies at the same time. The chicks here are generally a few days or even weeks old, so they'll have a better survival rate than day-old chicks. The store probably won't know the sex, and may not know the breed or vaccination status of the birds. If you're not allowed to keep roosters in your area, this could be a problem. In addition, farm stores aren't the cleanest areas, so it's possible the birds could be incubating an illness.

Asking farmers if they know anyone with chickens for sale seems obvious, but it's often overlooked. If you have a nearby farmers' market, that's an easy place to start searching. Anyone is able to sell chickens and eggs through eBay and similar sites, so if the seller has a good reputation and lives close enough for you to pick your eggs or chickens up, it might be worth a try. If they'll be posting eggs or chickens, it's risky. Don't forget; you're dealing with living creatures, not inanimate objects.

Regardless of where you buy your chickens, you need to ask the seller some questions before you buy. At this stage, they know more about their chickens than you do, so take advantage of that and take notes. Here are some example questions you should be asking yourself, and the seller:

- How long has the seller been raising chickens?
- What breeds do they have available?
- What sort of personality do the available breeds normally have?
- Are there any special precautions you need to take with these breeds?
- Are they especially sensitive to heat or cold?
- When do they normally start laying, how many eggs do they normally lay, and how long do they lay eggs consistently?
- Are the birds vaccinated? If so, which vaccinations, and can they provide vaccination certificates?
- How old are the birds?
- What feed are they used to? Can you buy a bag of it?

Even for experienced folk, it's difficult to tell the sex of a chicken. If you see straight run chickens for sale, it means you won't know the sex of the chicken when you buy it. The four main ways to sex chickens are venting, feather sexing, comb color, and behavior. The accuracy of any method depends on your experience and how familiar you are with the particular breed. Some breeds are easier to sex than others.

A chicken's vent is the opening where droppings and eggs come out. Venting, or vent sexing, involves squeezing a chick until feces are expelled from the vent, and their inner parts are visible. If the chick is male, you'll see a very small bulb inside. It requires a lot of skill to do this without killing the chick, and even the most experienced sexers aren't 100% accurate. Professional hatcheries use this method as it's the most accurate.

Feather sexing is much easier than venting, but you need to be around when the eggs hatch or shortly afterward. Female chicks usually have wing feathers before they hatch, while male chicks don't develop them until a few days after hatching. To check, you just have to stretch a chick's wing out and look for wing feathers. Female wing feathers will be different lengths, while male wing feathers will all appear the same length.

In some breeds, known as sex links, the down color of hen and rooster chicks are different. This makes it very easy to identify your hens and roosters. In other breeds, their comb size and color is an indication of their sex. This will only work if all of the chicks are the same breed, and you're familiar with that breed. Color varies by breed, but rooster chicks tend to have more pronounced combs than hens.

If you have more time to observe your chicks, behavior can be a giveaway. Rooster chicks often act more dominantly than hens, puffing up and approaching threats and novelty, rather than hiding in the corner. If you have multiple rooster chicks, you might see them "facing off" as if they're going to fight. Pecking order is important, and we'll get to that later!

If you're still not sure after several months, roosters will eventually crow and remove all doubt. While you're learning to sex chickens, you can use leg bands to mark which chicks you think are male and which are female. Once they're fully-grown, you can check your accuracy. Practice makes perfect.

You might come across several old wives' tales about sexing chickens. No matter what you hear, you can't tell the sex of a chicken by candling eggs, or by the shape of the egg.

When you're buying chickens in person, always ask to inspect the birds before you buy them. You can get a good indication of their state of health, temperament, and look for potential parasites during a quick inspection. A healthy chicken is active and alert. When you pick it up, it should feel plump and well-padded. A prominent breast bone is a sign that it's malnourished. Working from the head down, healthy laying hens have bright red combs. Blue combs indicate disease or organ problems. Particularly for roosters, scabs on their combs are a sign they've been fighting.

Healthy birds have clean, clear eyes with no bubbles in the corners, and they don't wheeze or cough. Avoid any birds with respiratory problems. The beak shouldn't be broken at the tip, flaking off, or crossed over, as those chickens will have trouble eating and drinking. Moving down, if the birds have lice, you'll see what look like tiny skin-colored grains of rice on their feathers and skin. The lice move quickly to avoid light. Northern fowl mites look like specks of dirt around the vent. Lice and mites are easily treatable, so don't consider them a deal-breaker, but they always make me question how well the seller has been looking after their birds.

If the feathers around the vent are excessively mucky, it can signify that the bird has worms or a condition called pasted-vent. This is where the dirty feathers completely seal the vent. This can be fatal. Again, these conditions are signs that the bird hasn't been well cared for. Missing feathers can be a sign of molting (in which case they're already stressed, and it's not a good time for them to move house) or bullying by other birds. Bullying is a sign that a bird is low in the pecking order, which could be either a result of a timid personality or a sign of illness. Raised scales on legs and feet are a sign of scaly leg mite. Bent toes are a genetic deformity. There's nothing wrong with bent-toed birds, but you shouldn't use them for breeding. If you see pinkish-red rough areas, redness, sores, or inflammation anywhere on the chicken's feet, they may have bumblefoot. This is treatable, but if a chicken's had it once, it's likely to recur.

The same principles apply to chicks. Healthy chicks are alert, active, bright-eyed, upright, and have no trouble walking. They'll move away from you when you approach. The physical checks are the same for chicks as for older chickens.

If you're buying chickens in person, don't forget to take a box or a carrier with slots for ventilation. Please avoid putting your chickens in the closed boot/trunk of your car, or you might sadly get home with a box of dead chickens. When you arrive home with your new chickens, remember that they'll already be stressed and confused. Don't make it worse. Quietly take their box to the coop, open the box, and leave it in the coop with the coop door locked. They'll come out and explore when they're ready. Make sure they have food, water, and treats waiting for them when they do leave the box.

When you check on them a few hours later, hopefully they'll be roosting happily. If any are still in the box, lift them out one at a time and place them on the roosting perch. Leave them in the coop for the first twenty-four hours. This teaches them that the coop is their home. When you let them out, they'll willingly return to the coop to roost.

After twenty-four hours, top-up their water, scatter some feed in the run, and open the coop door. Again, they'll come out when they're ready. If it takes more than a few hours, it's okay to give the timid chickens a bit of a push out into the run, then leave them to explore. Chickens can get into trouble quickly in a new place, so check on them regularly. You can expect overturned water containers, heads stuck in interesting holes, and similar misfortunes. Make sure you fix any problems they find!

As sunset approaches, make sure your chickens have returned to the coop. They may do this without prompting, but if not, gently encourage them back towards the coop. For the first week, you might need to encourage them to go out in the morning and back in the evening, but they'll learn the routine soon enough. Once they know the routine, you can start letting them free-range and even introduce them to your pets and children if you want to. If you have dogs, keep them on a leash at first. If your chickens are settling in properly, you'll soon see the normal signs of happy, healthy chickens. Clucking, searching for bugs, and dust baths are good signs, while constant pacing and squawking are signs that something could be amiss.

Chapter 5 - Food, Water & Nutrition Need-To-Knows

Proper nutrition is the key to a long, healthy life for your chickens and lots of high-quality eggs, for you. While traditionally chickens lived off bugs, grains, and kitchen scraps, we now know a whole lot more about chicken nutrition. The main feeding concerns you might have are what to feed them, how often, and how much. Just as with humans, overeating leads to obesity and health problems, including back, joint, and heart problems. If you're raising broilers, this is less of a concern, but egg-laying hens need to stay healthy for several years. Too much protein causes kidney problems, while too little restricts growth. Insufficient calcium leads to thin eggs that break easily.

We'll start with what to feed them - and what to avoid. Chicken feed can be divided into pellets, forage, scraps, treats, grit, and supplements. Like us, chickens need a balanced diet of protein, carbohydrates, fats, vitamins, and minerals. Pellets are the basic feed for chickens, and they're formulated to suit chickens of different ages and types. You should look for a good quality commercial pellets appropriate for the age and type of your chickens.

Chick crumbs are high-protein feed for chicks that are roughly five weeks old and under. Chick crumbs are about 19% protein, which helps the chicks to grow. Special broiler bird starter feed is available for meat bird chicks. Medicated chick crumbs can help to prevent coccidiosis, a common disease caused by a parasite that attaches itself to the intestinal lining. This isn't necessary if your chicks have been vaccinated against coccidiosis, or if you keep your chicks in a clean, spacious brooder.

From six weeks onwards, pullets are still growing. They need growers pellets or growers mash, which is roughly 16% protein. Laying hens need layers pellets or layers mash. The protein in layers pellets/mash is around 16%, as with growers pellets/mash, but it also includes other nutrients and minerals to support egg production. If you're planning to use your hens for breeding as well as laying, look for breeders pellets or breeders mash.

Given the opportunity to forage, chickens will supplement their diet with more protein (bugs, slugs, worms, and other similar tasty morsels) and whatever they can find in your garden. This isn't always healthy. Bear in mind that chickens are often smarter than what we give them credit for. If they refuse to eat something, they're probably right. Chickens love all sorts of scraps of unprocessed foods, especially fruit, vegetables, and grains. It's a great way to keep them happy, reduce waste, and cut your feed bill at the same time. However, there are a few things that are safe for humans, but which are definitely not for them.

I shouldn't need to say this, but please don't use pesticides, herbicides, or other toxic chemicals on plants which your chickens are likely to consume. This includes weed killer, slug repellent, rat poison, and anything else that's designed to kill plants or animals deliberately.

All processed foods are out, along with anything too salty, sweet, spicy, deep-fried, or caffeinated. This means no chocolate, curry, tea, or pickles for your chickens, but let's be honest: who really throws chocolate out? As well as chocolate and processed food, several common foods aren't good for chickens. Most of these won't kill them in small amounts, but they can have some very nasty cumulative effects on either your chickens' health or their eggs. This seems obvious, but while stale, overripe, or wilted food is fine, don't feed your chickens moldy food of any sort.

Other <u>food scraps and leftovers to avoid</u> feeding your chickens are:
- Alcohol
- Apple, cherry, peach, pear and plum seeds and leaves
- Avocado
- Citrus fruit and peel
- Raw eggs. They're not a health risk, but once you teach them that raw eggs are food, they're more likely to start eating their eggs.
- Onions, regardless of color
- Peanuts
- Rhubarb plant or leaves
- Raw dried beans and uncooked rice (cooked or sprouted beans and rice are fine)
- Tomato and eggplant/aubergine leaves. People say that ripe tomatoes are probably okay, but I prefer not to risk it.
- White potatoes (sweet potatoes are fine).
- Spinach can interfere with calcium absorption, but isn't a problem in small amounts, while large quantities of iceberg

lettuce and dairy products may cause diarrhea.
- Some types of foods won't harm your chickens but will taint their eggs. Asparagus, garlic, fish and fishmeal, and cat food fall in this category. Some people find that broccoli, cauliflower, and Brussels sprouts have a similar effect.

Toxins don't always kill immediately. They can build up slowly until they reach a dangerous level. Even if you can't see obvious symptoms, toxins can reduce lifespan or quality of life. Depending on the level of the specific toxin in the chicken, **symptoms of poisoning can include:**

- poor egg quality;
- fewer eggs;
- diarrhea;
- rapid heart rate;
- convulsions;
- gout;
- kidney failure;
- internal congestion; and

- hemorrhaging.

If any of your chickens are exhibiting some of these symptoms, move the rest of your flock back to the pen - and take the sick chicken to the vet.

It's not all doom and gloom in the garden. Some garden herbs and flowers are actually beneficial to your chickens. **Popular healthy flowers include:**

- Calendula
- Echinacea
- Geraniums
- Hibiscus
- Hollyhock
- Impatiens
- Lilac
- Marigolds
- Nasturtium
- Pansy
- Pea Blossoms
- Peony
- Phlox

- Roses
- Snap Dragon
- Squash Blossom
- Sunflower
- Violet

Chapter 8 explains which plants to avoid feeding to your chickens.

Almost all **common herbs are either safe or beneficial for chickens.** These include:

- Basil
- Bay Leaves
- Calendula
- Catnip
- Cayenne Pepper
- Chamomile
- Cilantro
- Cinnamon
- Comfrey
- Dill
- Fennel
- Feverfew

- Garlic
- Ginger
- Lavender
- Lemon Balm
- Marjoram
- Mint
- Nettles
- Oregano
- Parsley
- Peppermint
- Rosemary
- Sage
- Tarragon
- Thyme
- Wormwood
- Yarrow

There are mixed reports about chicken consumption of coriander, so you're better off avoiding that. Furthermore, you can hang bunches of dried herbs around your coop to help freshen it up, if you like.

Several flowers that we consider weeds are surprisingly very nutritious for your chickens. Since you're not using pesticides, herbicides, or other chemicals on your lawn and plants (at least, I hope you're not - they're not good for your chickens!), it's reassuring to know that there's some benefit to having some weeds around.

Between them, dandelion, chickweed, and clover are excellent sources of vitamins A, B, C, E, K, and iron. These help with respiratory and circulatory health. Chickweed is a natural analgesic and supports digestive health. **Some other helpful weeds are:**

- Bitter Cress
- Evening Primrose
- Hawkweed
- Mugwort
- Oxalis
- Plantain
- Yellow dock

While kitchen scraps are popular with chickens, they absolutely love scratch and cracked corn. Treats are a great way to both tame your chickens and encourage them to forage. Scratch is a mixture of grains, including corn, oats, wheat, and rye, while cracked corn is corn that's been broken into small pieces. Adult chickens can also eat whole corn. Bear in mind that corn and scratch are high in fat, so keep it as a treat. If you scatter one handful per hen, that's more than enough. Also bear in mind that if you have white birds and want to exhibit them, feeding them corn can give their feathers a yellowish hue.

High-quality feed should contain almost everything your chickens need. As with humans, supplements should support a healthy diet, not replace one. That said, if any of your chickens seem a bit under the weather, certain supplements may help. You can find more detail on symptoms and treatments for the most common nutrient deficiencies in Chapter 9.

Insoluble grit is an essential supplement for chickens of all ages. Grit is a technical name for fine dirt and rocks. It helps to break up food in the *gizzard*. If they don't have enough grit, chickens can develop digestive disorders. Free-range chickens can easily get enough grit by foraging, especially if you allow them to roam in a natural dirt area. Don't mix grit with your birds' feed - just leave a container of it nearby. They'll take what they need.

As with humans, electrolytes in water can help with heat, dehydration, and illness. You can buy packaged electrolytes in most feed stores. Probiotics help to increase the beneficial bacteria in the gut, helping chickens digest food. Healthy, well-fed chickens shouldn't need probiotics, but probiotics can help chickens who are on antibiotics for an infection.

Herbs and natural products can help solve several issues in your chickens. Fresh or powdered garlic can help with some infections and worm infestations. If you're using it for worms, remember it's a supplement. Use it alongside a proper worm treatment, not instead of one. Mix one tablespoon per gallon of feed. Molasses contains iron and other minerals. More usefully, when you add it to feed with other supplements, it increases the intake of the other supplements by making them stick to the feed. Add a quarter of a cup per gallon of feed, and mix it well. A tablespoon of cinnamon or Epsom salts per gallon of feed can help with diarrhea. Three tablespoons of aloe Vera per gallon of water can help with coccidiosis.

Calcium is an essential supplement for laying hens. Calcium is usually provided as oyster shells, which the chickens can play with, as well as eat. Insufficient calcium can lead to weak-shelled eggs and even weak bones. If a hen doesn't have enough calcium, her body will start extracting it from her bones to make eggshells. Start offering hens oyster shells in a separate container from about sixteen weeks of age. They'll take what they need. Just like us, if chickens don't get enough sunlight, they'll need vitamin D supplements. If you live in an area that doesn't get much daylight in winter, consider a vitamin D3 supplement. Kelp is a popular choice, but see what's available at your local feed store.

There are two schools of thought for how to feed your chickens:

Free choice; Free choice feeding leaves food available to your chickens whenever they want it. This system assumes that your chickens know what and how much to eat. This is generally true, and free choice is the most popular way to feed chickens - and the easiest.

Scheduled; Scheduled feeding means setting their food out at particular times, and removing it when the scheduled feeding period is over. The disadvantage of this is that you have to stick to a set schedule each and every day.

No matter which feeding system you use, ensure there is enough space at the feeders for all the birds to get enough food. This is especially critical for scheduled feeding. If any birds are missing out, provide more feeders, or some chickens will end up malnourished. Putting feeders both inside and outside the coop gives all of your chickens a chance to eat, including the less dominant ones. If you only have one feeding station, bullies are likely to stop the more timid chickens from eating.

If you're raising chicks, there are a few special considerations. You should make sure chicks have access to food at all times. Chick feeders are specifically designed with small holes to prevent waste, as well as a gravity feed to keep the feeder topped up. As with full-grown chickens, chicks need a separate container of grit. Chick grit is finer than grit for adult chickens. When your chicks are about 3/4 grown, they can transition to adult grit. For the first few days, sprinkle the chicks' feed on a white plate or white paper towel. They're naturally curious, so they'll find it easily. Once they realize it's food, you can slowly transition it to the feeder.

When you calculate feed quantities, work on one cup or 1/4 pound of pellets per adult chicken per day. On average, they tend to eat more in winter and less in summer. Large-breed chickens sometimes eat grit until they're full. This causes obvious problems, as there's no room left for food. If this happens, limit their grit. If you have to change your chickens' diet, or when you first bring them home, change their feed gradually. Mix-in increasing amounts of the new feed with the old feed over a few weeks.

Chickens obviously need clean drinking water. An average adult laying hen needs at least a pint of water daily. In summer, you can increase this to a quart. (about 1.1 Litres) Meat chickens and large breeds need even more than that. Water should always be free-choice. An ideal waterer will be clean, protected from debris, free of mold and algae, and installed at a height where the chickens don't have to bend down to access the water. In summer, keep the waterer in the shade; and in winter, a heater will make sure it doesn't freeze. As with their food, having multiple waterers will ensure that all your chickens have easy access to water. If you can, put at least one in the run, and one where they free-range. While chicks also need water, it's essential to choose a narrow, shallow container so that they can't drown. When you put the chicks into the brooder, dip their beaks into the water so that they know where to find it.

Chapter 6 – The Story of the Egg & All about Laying

Fresh eggs are one of the leading reasons for keeping chickens. Even if you've never kept a chicken, you've almost certainly eaten an egg. This chapter covers everything you never realized you needed to know about eggs, and we'll start by answering the question, "What is an egg?"

<u>Whether an egg is fertilized or unfertilized, it consists of seven basic parts:</u>

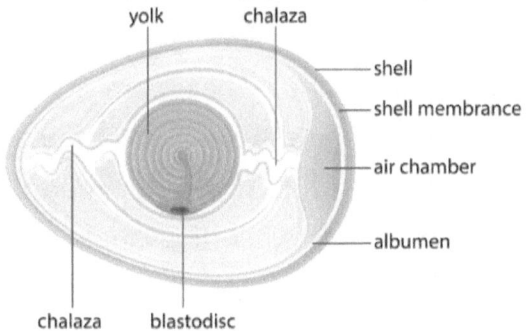

shell;
membranes;
albumen (the white);
yolk (the yellow/orange part);
germinal disc;
chalazae; and an
air sac.

Each part plays an essential function in supporting a developing chick.

The shell protects the contents of the egg. It's a semipermeable membrane, mostly made from calcium carbonate. It's covered by a membrane called the bloom (or cuticle) that blocks contaminants from entering the shell.

Inside, the shell is lined with **two membranes**: the outer shell membrane; and the inner shell membrane. These are made from keratin and work with the shell and the cuticle to keep contaminants out. The outer membrane is attached to the shell, while the inner membrane attaches to the albumen.

The albumen, often known as "the egg white" comes next. It contains vitamins, minerals, protein, and water for a developing chick, and it protects the yolk.

The yolk is the yellow or orange part in the middle of the egg, where a developing chick would grow. This is high in nutrients, including vitamins A and D, phosphorous, calcium, thiamine, and riboflavin.

The germinal disc is also called the egg cell or blastodisc. It's where the sperm enters the egg, and it sits on the surface of the yolk. In a fertilized egg, this is where the embryo starts to form.

Chalazae (plural) are strings of twisted tissue at opposite ends of the yolk. They stabilize the yolk and the germinal disc.

The air sac forms between the inner and outer membranes when the contents of a freshly laid egg cool and contract. Over time, moisture and carbon dioxide leave the egg, air enters to replace them, and the air sac expands.

The next relevant question is, how do hens make eggs? Believe it or not, it all starts with the sun. It takes roughly fourteen hours of sunlight to trigger the hormonal changes required for a hen to release an egg from their ovary into the uterus. The uterus fills with albumen, and a calcium membrane forms around the albumen on the inside of the uterus. This membrane will become the shell. If the hen doesn't have the protein, calcium, vitamins, and minerals to form the albumen and the shell, she won't be able to make a healthy egg. From the arrival of the yolk in the uterus, it takes around twenty-six hours for the egg to become fully-formed. At this stage, the uterus contracts, pushing the egg out of the vent.

Once you understand how eggs are formed, it's clear why nutrition is crucially important for laying hens. When you watch your hens, you'll notice several typical behaviors, starting an hour or two before laying. These are: searching for a good place to lay an egg, selecting a good nesting site, and forming a nest hollow. Some breeds and individuals do this more obviously than others. Once you're familiar with your hens' habits, you'll be able to predict when you can collect the eggs.

If the hen can't find a good place to lay or is distracted, she'll sometimes stop searching and just lay the egg wherever she happens to be. This often happens with less-dominant hens when dominant hens are taking up all of the available nesting boxes. Most hens prefer to lay eggs in nests or nesting boxes, but one or two will always lay in other places. If you know roughly when they're likely to lay, you have a stronger chance of finding any missing eggs. Finding eggs laid outside nesting boxes is likely to take longer, and they're more likely to be damaged, contaminated, or even broken and eaten. If you don't collect the eggs promptly after they're laid, your hens might turn broody or start eating the eggs.

Most hens lay eggs in the early morning or within six hours of sunrise, but the twenty-six-hour cycle makes it difficult for them to stick to a strict schedule. It's very rare for a hen to lay at night. Because there's less sun in winter, it might not be enough to trigger laying. This means hens may not lay at all in winter, or laying might be irregular.

While some breeds are more reliable layers than others, there are still some steps you can take to optimize egg production/egg quality for any breed…

The most obvious point is that chickens less than three years old lay more eggs than older chickens. All laying hens need around fourteen hours of sunlight to trigger egg production, so you have more chance of eggs if they spend as much time outside as possible. While you can use artificial light to force egg laying in winter, this isn't good for your hens; they need a break, too. Let nature do it's thing. Free-range chickens typically lay more eggs, and more nutritious eggs. If you want to breed your chickens, consider keeping hens specifically for brooding and raising chicks. Not all egg-laying breeds are also good brooders.

The main rules to follow for gathering eggs are to gather early, and gather often. If you can, check twice a day. For your own health, it's vital that you gather the eggs before they have a chance to get dirty. As well as reducing contamination, this also minimizes the amount of egg-cleaning to do later. Use a clean basket or plastic container to collect the eggs, and don't stack them more than five-high, or the eggs on the bottom can crack. Keep them at a constant temperature until you wash them. If they cool down too quickly, the shell will contract and contamination can enter the egg.

Start by collecting the unattended eggs, then gently lift any hens out of their nests, remove the eggs, and put the hens on the roosts. At the same time, check the nesting boxes. If they're soiled with droppings or broken eggs, clean them out, and replace the bedding.

In fact, there are **three main schools of thought about egg cleaning**: dry, wet, and don't bother! If possible, dry cleaning is a better choice because it leaves the antibacterial cuticle intact. If the cuticle is intact, then you don't have to refrigerate the eggs. Dry cleaning involves wiping dirt and droppings from the egg with a scourer, loofah, or similar. Some people even use fine sandpaper to remove all traces of contamination, but this can also damage the cuticle.

If the eggs are very dirty or have yolk on the shells, wet cleaning may be unavoidable. Use running water that's warmer than the egg, but not hot, to gently wash each egg. Wet cleaning causes the shell to expand and push dirt out of the pores. When you do this, you'll often feel the cuticle come off - it feels slimy. When the egg is clean, dry it with a paper towel, place it in a clean carton, then, if you wish, sanitize the eggs by spraying them with diluted bleach.

Some people don't worry about cleaning the eggs at all. Whichever method you use, once your eggs are clean and dry, label them in pencil with the date of collection before storing them.

If you didn't wet-clean your eggs, you can leave them at room temperature for at least a month. You can keep them in any container that protects the eggs; egg cartons are cheap and convenient. You can refrigerate them if you want, but it's not required. Wet-cleaned eggs have no cuticle to protect them so, if you're not using them immediately, they have to stay in the fridge. Eggs kept in an airtight container in the refrigerator can last up to six months, while those in an egg carton will last around a month.

If you can, store your eggs pointy-end-down. The air sac at the blunt end helps to reduce moisture loss, which keeps the egg fresh for longer. People have had varying success increasing their eggs' shelf-life by coating them with assorted substances, ranging from petroleum jelly to lime juice. As long as you stick with non-toxic substances and check the egg before using it, it can't hurt to experiment!

Cooking with eggs

When you're cooking with eggs, there are a couple of tips and tricks to make your life easier. If you want to make boiled eggs, use your older eggs; they're easier to peel than fresh eggs. If you need to separate the eggs and yolk, refrigerate the eggs first, but if you want to beat the whites, it's easier if the eggs are at room temperature.

Here are my favorite recipes to use up eggs: frittata, quiche, omelet, scrambled eggs, banana pancakes, and peanut butter choc chip cookies. The main meals all use the same basic process of breaking eggs, mixing them, and adding whichever bits and pieces you have in your fridge. The others are just fast, fun, and tasty.

To check how fresh an egg is, place it in a bowl of water. Old eggs float on the surface, eggs a few weeks old just start to rise off the bottom of the container, and fresh eggs sink. Just because an egg floats, it doesn't mean it's spoiled. Crack it into a cup before you add it to a recipe, and your nose will immediately tell you if it's not safe to use. When you find a spoiled egg (and we all do, sooner or later), you can just put it on your compost heap.

Egg fertilization

When an egg is fertilized, the blastodisc (germinal disc) becomes known as the blastoderm. If incubated in the right conditions, the blastoderm develops into an embryo, then a chick. After twenty-one days, it will be fully developed and ready to hatch.

There are two ways to identify a fertilized egg. The method you choose depends very much on why you want to know if it's fertilized. The simplest option is to break open the egg and examine the contents. A fertile egg has a small white "bullseye" on the yolk. It looks like two white circles, one inside the other.

If the reason you want to know if it's fertile is that you want to hatch that specific egg, breaking it clearly isn't ideal. In this case, candling would be the better option.

Candling involves shining a bright light under the blunt end of an egg that's been incubating for a few days. White and light-colored eggs are the easiest to candle. If the egg is fertile, you'll see a dark spot in the middle, surrounded by spider-like veins. In an unfertilized egg, you'll see only the shape of the yolk.

Once set (placed in the incubator, or under a broody hen), chicks take twenty-one days to develop, although some will hatch a day or two early, or late. When you decide to hatch eggs, don't forget that about half of your chicks will be roosters. If you don't want to keep roosters (or you're not allowed to keep them in your area), make sure you have a plan for what to do with the unwanted chicks.

When you select eggs to incubate, choose the even, undamaged eggs and don't wash them. Ideally, they should be set within a week of being laid. While you're waiting to set them, keep them in a cool place and turn them daily to keep the yolk centered. If you ordered your eggs online, leave them upright with the blunt end up for twenty-four hours before setting to let the contents settle.

About a week before you plan to set your eggs, wash the incubator with a 10% bleach solution, then rewash it with warm soapy water before rinsing it thoroughly. Once it's clean and dry, put it somewhere with a stable ambient temperature, turn it on and test it. Before you add the eggs, the temperature should be steady in the incubator. When measured at the top of the eggs, an incubator with a fan should have a temperature of 95.5-100F, while one without a fan should have a temperature of 101–102F. To start with, the humidity should be somewhere between 28-50%.

Once you're happy that your incubator is working, put the eggs into the incubator, blunt end up. If you mark each egg's blunt end with a pencil mark or a number, it will make your life easier. For the first eighteen days, turn the eggs an odd number of times, each day. The marks will help you to keep track of which eggs you've turned. Make sure they are different ends up, each night. Without regular turning, the embryo tends to stick to the shell membrane, which causes abnormal growth.

On days four and ten, candle the eggs as you turn them to see how they're developing. Make a note if there's no sign of development by day ten, then check again on day fourteen. You can discard any eggs with no sign of development by day fourteen. While candling, don't keep the egg out of the incubator for more than five or ten minutes and don't candle them all at once, or the incubator will lose too much heat.

The last few days of incubation, days eighteen to twenty-one, are known as "lockdown." When lockdown starts on day eighteen, increase the humidity to 65-75%, leave the eggs blunt-end up, and don't open the incubator unless it's absolutely necessary. The air bubble in the blunt end of the egg is a breathing space for the chick when it hatches. The drier the outside air is, the faster the moisture from the egg evaporates, and the faster the bubble grows. Maintaining the correct humidity stops the bubble from growing too much or staying too small, and ensures that the chick can breathe.

When the eggs start hatching, don't try to help. Chicks are sometimes still attached to the shell by blood vessels. If you pull these off, it can cause fatal bleeding. Chicks normally take five to seven hours to hatch, but some take up to twenty-four hours. The peeping of chicks can encourage unhatched eggs to start hatching. Once they've all hatched, lower the temperature to about 95F. Let them dry off and fluff up in the incubator, then gently move them to the brooder. This process will take six to twelve hours.

The chicks will fortunately have absorbed enough yolk during the hatching process to keep them alive for a few days, but they'll still need water in the brooder. After a day or two, offer them free-choice food. If some eggs don't hatch, leave them in the incubator until day twenty-three, and candle any unhatched eggs before deciding to discard them.

Chicks are cute, but they grow rapidly. You'll need to keep them safe and warm in a brooder for about four weeks. They'll need warmth, safety, food, water, and fine grit. Two ways to provide these are either in a brooder, or with a broody hen. Broodiness has been bred out of most chickens, but if you happen to have a broody hen or two, they'll do a great job of looking after your chicks. If one of your hens is broody while your eggs are incubating, encourage her. Leave golf balls or smooth stones under her and see if she looks after them. A few days before hatching, move the hen and her nest into a dog crate on the floor of the coop.

When the chicks are a day old, take them out and let her hear them peeping, then tuck them, one at a time, under the hen. If she starts clucking, pushing the chicks further underneath her, and trying to protect them, you're winning! For each chick she accepts, remove one "egg." Keep an eye on them for a few hours to make sure she really has accepted them and to make sure the chicks understand that they're safe and warm under her wings. Always keep your brooder ready as a backup.

Some people prefer to introduce the chicks at night, while the hens are sleeping. The advantage of this is that chickens can't track either time or eggs, so she might think the chicks just hatched overnight. The downside is that, if she doesn't accept the chicks, you might come back in the morning and find some dead chicks. If the hen accepts the chicks, it'll make your life much easier. She'll raise them, teach them what to eat and how to behave, and introduce them to the rest of the flock.

If you don't have a broody hen, you'll need a brooder. While your eggs are on lockdown in the incubator, it's time to set up and check your brooder. Many people successfully use paddling pools; feeding troughs; large cardboard, wooden or plastic boxes; and fish tanks. Whatever you use, the brooder needs walls, a floor you can cover with bedding, somewhere to put food and water, and a heat lamp.

It should be big enough to allow about two to four square feet per chick, and it's better if it's round or oval rather than square or rectangular. If it's less than a foot deep, you'll also need a cover to stop the chicks escaping. Fine netting or chicken wire works perfectly. If your brooder has corners, block them with cardboard to prevent the chicks from packing into the corners and suffocating. Your heat lamp should be in only one corner/side of your brooder so the chicks can move away if they get too hot. Keep it at least twenty inches above the bedding, and preferably at least three feet away from the walls. A 250-watt infrared lamp with a red bulb, a reflector, a wire guard, and a mounting clamp is ideal. If the lamp falls into the brooder, the wire guard reduces the chance that it will set fire to the bedding.

To adjust the temperature, you'll need some way to adjust the lamp's height from the floor of the brooder. This will depend heavily on your setup, but a hanging chain and an s-hook are quite versatile and easy to adjust. In order to monitor the temperature, set up a thermometer with a remote sensor. Put the sensor under the heat lamp, with the readout at the edge of the brooder, where you can easily read it. When the chicks first move in, the temperature under the lamp should be about 95F. You can reduce this by 5F per week.

Once your chicks move into the brooder, watch how they behave. If they start crowding under the heat lamp, it's too cold. Move the heat lamp down, or add an extra lamp. Alternatively, if they spend all their time as far from the lamp as possible, it's probably too hot. Adjust it until they seem comfortable. To help with growth during the first week, leave the lights on for at least eighteen hours a day, or as long as twenty-two hours. After this, you can gradually reduce the time to sixteen hours.

We touched on bedding in Chapter 3, but you'll need appropriate absorbent bedding for your chicks. Newspaper is too slippery, and the aromatic oils in cedar shavings will irritate your chicks' lungs and make them prone to respiratory problems. One or two inches of pine shavings on the bottom of the brooder is cheap and effective. Whatever you use, don't forget to change it regularly, or whenever it starts to smell.

We covered food covered in detail earlier, so I'll stick to feeders here. As a guide, you'll need four inches of feeder space per chick. A clean egg carton works well for young chicks, but as they grow, it's worth buying a commercial feeder that's designed to keep droppings out of their food. After the first couple of days, you should always offer your chicks free-choice food and fine grit. Remember, they're growing fast! When they're eight weeks old, start changing gradually to grower feed. Mix it with the starter feed and increase the proportion of grower:starter feed over a few weeks. This gives them a chance to adjust to the taste of the new food. From week eighteen, you can start changing to appropriate adult feed. If you have leftover starter feed, either use it up or throw it out. It tends to go moldy after long, which could unfortunately kill any future chicks.

The two main concerns with waterers are providing sufficient water and stopping your chicks from drowning in the water. Chicks are clumsy, and can easily fall into the waterers. To avoid this, use a shallow dish with clean pebbles or marbles spread around in it. The chicks can easily drink from the space in between the pebbles.

Chicks don't need treats until they've learned what regular food is. You can start introducing occasional healthy treats during the second week. Finely chopped hard-boiled eggs or sweetcorn make tasty treats for chicks, while whole lettuce leaves hanging in the brooder give them something to play with. After a few more weeks, start introducing kitchen scraps, but continue to chop them up into a sensible size for the chicks.

Hens will typically stop laying eggs for one of three reasons:

Either, the hen is not getting enough sunlight, is old, or will stop laying due to stress/health problems.

As discussed earlier, it takes about fourteen hours of sunlight to trigger the release of an egg. If it's winter, this is the most likely reason your hens aren't laying. Hens start laying when they're about eighteen to twenty weeks old and continue until they're about two or three years old, although this varies by breed. If a young hen stops laying and it's not winter, it may be down to health problems. The main health problem that stops hens from laying is stress. There's not much you can do about stress from molting, but you can address other direct causes of stress. Make sure they're not overcrowded, are safe from predators, are not too hot or cold, are not being bullied by other chickens, and that there are no loud noises around the coop.

Poor nutrition is the next common reason for decreased egg production. This can be because of insufficient supplements, or too many treats. Double-check that the hen has access to oyster shells. that she isn't being kept away from the feeder by bullies, and that she isn't eating too many treats. A ratio of around 90% feed to 10% treats generally works well, I find.

Chapter 7 – Chicken Psychology & The Pecking Order

Regardless of what you've heard, while chickens may be 'bird-brained', they're not stupid. Multiple studies have shown chickens follow complex social rules, use varied sounds for communication, and have demonstrated intelligence in some areas that are equivalent to a primate or even a human child. Ignore these revelations at your own peril!

You won't have to watch your chickens for long to get a sense of their personalities. Regardless of their breed, their personality can vary from timid to inquisitive, from cheeky to bully - just as our temperaments do. As well as personality, scientists have demonstrated that chickens have a sense of numbers and time, can anticipate future events, and can perform basic addition and subtraction. They can even reason by simple deduction, a skill that human children don't develop until age seven. In the chicken equivalent of the marshmallow test (a well-known test of children's ability to defer gratification for an improved reward) - the chickens will wait longer for a better food reward. When it comes to tracking moving balls, their performance is similar to most primates. Chickens are able to remember the trajectory of a hidden ball for up to three minutes if they could see the ball moving, and up to one minute if they couldn't see it. [Vallortigara et al. 1998]

Chicken communication involves assorted visual displays, and at least twenty-four distinct sounds to indicate information including alarm, distress, laying eggs, mating, and more. Watch your chickens for long enough, and you'll see them deceive each other, learn from each other, and teach each other. It shouldn't be any surprise that an intelligent, social species such as chickens can behave like this.

For any species, hierarchy and social rules are a normal part of living in a social group.

Chickens are no different. Back in 1921, Thorleif Schjelderup-Ebbe came up with the term "pecking order" to describe flock hierarchy. The term stuck. The term "pecking order" is an accurate description of how the hierarchy is determined and enforced: by pecking. You need to understand and actively manage the pecking order, or things will get messy in your flock. At best, chickens will get hurt; and at worst, killed.

The pecking order is akin to a military hierarchy. Every chicken is ranked from the top down. Bigger, stronger chickens bully their way to the top; while quiet, submissive, sick, or injured chickens fall to the bottom. The pecking order determines access to food, water, dust baths, nesting boxes, and location on the roosting perch.

The chicken at the top is responsible for safety. They're constantly on the watch for danger. When a predator appears, they usher the flock to safety. When they find a food source, they usually let the other chickens eat while they keep watch. This ensures the survival of the flock.

Pecking order is usually set early, then rarely changes. If you have one rooster, he'll be at the top, with the hens ranked below him. Once you understand this, you can use it in your flock management. If one of your chickens is ill or injured, you need to separate them from the flock until they recover, or they'll be a target for higher-ranked chickens.

Bullies are often in the middle of the pecking order. The best way to solve bullying is to separate the bully in a segregation pen for a few days. When they return to the flock, the pecking order will have changed, and they'll rejoin at the bottom. If bullies team up, do the same but return them to the flock on separate days.

Don't forget: you're also part of the pecking order. You're at the top, above the head chicken. Hens generally respect that; but some roosters will challenge you for the top spot. Donning leather gloves and pinning the rooster down whenever they attack usually solves the problem. If not, I've found that rooster stew has a 100% success rate! (it's a joke)

The key to a manageable pecking order is sufficient space. If you have enough space in the coop and run, enough roosting space, enough nesting boxes, enough feeders, and enough waterers, the flock is more likely to be peaceful. Providing places for chickens to hide if they want to, also helps. Hanging feeders and waterers in the middle of a space rather than in the corners makes it easier for your chickens to access them and reduces bickering over access.

Buying vs. Breeding?
At first, the trade-off between buying and breeding chickens seems straightforward: buying appears simple and less work; breeding seems more complicated and more work. But breeding isn't actually that complicated, especially if you have broody hens. I explained the process of hatching eggs in Chapter 6, so in this chapter, I'll

focus on getting fertilized eggs from your chickens. If you have a choice, aim for springtime. While you can breed at any time, in Spring, you'll have more eggs to choose from. I hope this is obvious, but to get fertilized eggs, you'll need a rooster to mate with the hen or hens.

You might want to breed just to increase your flock, to improve your breed, or to develop a show breed. You'll need to choose your breeding birds with your goal in mind. Regardless of your reason for breeding, always chose healthy chickens that meet your goals and have decent temperaments. If you want to develop a breed or show birds, choose breeding birds that have the characteristics which you want to enhance and pass on to their young.

Once you've selected your breeding birds, keep your chosen rooster with your chosen hens. If all chickens involved are healthy and active, nature will take its course with no further prompting. Chicken mating can look quite aggressive at the best of times, and over-enthusiastic roosters can injure hens. During mating, the rooster jumps on the hen's back, grabs her by the comb or the back of the head with his beak, and stabilizes himself with his feet while he, 'does the deed'. If your rooster is injuring your hens, consider changing roosters. After mating, it will take at least two weeks for the hens to start laying fertilized eggs. Check the eggs regularly, and when you have fertilized eggs, you can move on to the incubator process described previously.

Whenever you add new chickens to your flock, you upset the current pecking order. If you do it without sufficient care, you'll end up with sick or injured chickens (at best) or dead chickens (at worst). There are two scenarios for introducing new chickens to your flock: adding chicks that you've bred or raised on-site, or adding pullets or adult chickens from a different flock. Whatever you do, before adding new chickens, make sure your coop is big enough for the combined flock. To be fair to your chickens, try not to mix breeds of drastically different size and temperament, and always introduce at least two new chickens at a time. Large breeds are more dominant and prone to bullying smaller breeds, and it's harder to bully two chickens than one.

Adding adult roosters is challenging, and often results in the death of the junior rooster. If you want multiple roosters, raise them together from chicks. If a broody hen raised your chicks, she'll introduce them to the flock herself, but if you raised them in a brooder, it's your job to ease them in. Start introducing the chicks when they're at least four weeks old - although six weeks would be preferred. They won't fully integrate into the flock until they're about ten to twelve weeks old and fully feathered.

At first, give the chicks their own coop and run alongside the flock, separated by wire. This lets the chicks and the chickens see and smell each other, but protects the chicks from any grumpy chickens wanting to cause trouble. Don't forget to keep feeding the chicks starter feed until they're sixteen to twenty weeks old - they're still growing! When the chicks are ten to twelve weeks old, let them out to free-range with the flock. This gives them room to escape any bullies. If free-ranging goes well, take the partition down during the day and let the chicks and chickens mingle in the run, but separate them at night. At this point, you'll need to change the whole flock over to starter feed as the calcium in layer feed will damage the chicks' kidneys. Don't forget to put out additional crushed oyster shells as a calcium supplement for the laying hens.

After a few weeks of this, remove the partition in the chicks' coop and move the chicks in with the flock. For the first few days, you might have to help the chicks work out where to go in the evening, and remember keep a close eye out for any injured birds. When you have new chickens from somewhere else, your primary concerns should be disease, infection, and parasites. Adult chickens are more likely to be carrying these sorts of things than chicks from a reputable hatchery.

To prevent the new chickens from spreading infection or disease to your flock, check them thoroughly for any signs of health problems as described in Chapter 4, then quarantine them in a separate coop and run for at least a week (a month is better). We're all pretty aware of what quarantine means now! (I'm writing this book for you during the infamous global pandemic of 2020)

While they're in quarantine, change them over to the feed you normally use and make sure they have sufficient supplements. Use the time to make sure they're as healthy as they can be before they join your flock. During this quarantine period, it's critical that you don't cross-contaminate either flock. Wash your hands, change your boots and clothes, and use separate equipment when caring for each flock. When the quarantine is over, the key to integrating the new chickens is to do it slowly, just like you do with chicks. Keep the new chickens in a pen alongside the main flock for at least a week so they can all get used to each other. After a week or so, let them free-range together, or let your main flock into the new chickens' pen.

Before you let the flocks free range together, make sure you're prepared to break up any chicken fights and treat injuries. Wear leather gloves, long sleeves, and sturdy jeans. Have a supply of towels, boxes, cages, and styptic powder ready. Chickens of any age are drawn to peck red things. This means that if a chicken's bleeding, other chickens will gang up and peck the wound. If you don't separate them, they can peck the injured chicken to death. Sometimes they then eat it. To avoid this, use treats and toys to distract them when you first let them free range together. A hay bale or hanging lettuce will give them something to focus on while they get used to each other.

When they start to mingle, they'll begin establishing the pecking order. As you know, this is normal. Don't interfere unless a chicken is injured or starts to bleed, but if a fight lasts more than five to ten minutes, separate the flocks and try again the following day. Keep doing this until they settle down within a few minutes of meeting. For aggressive breeds, this can take three or four days. When they can play nicely outside, you can let the new chickens move into the main coop. If they want to return to their own coop, let them. Once they're asleep, move them into the main coop. Keep an eye on the new chickens for a week or so after they join the main flock. Make sure they're eating, drinking, and settling in properly. It's normal for hens to stop laying for a while after joining a new flock, so don't worry too much about that.

Chapter 8 – Beware the Garden! (& The Predators)

As I've mentioned several times, chickens aren't stupid. Like most animals, they'll normally avoid eating things that will make them ill, they'll hide when they sense predators nearby, and if they need a particular nutrient, they'll be able to find something that contains it. You'll notice, I say, "normally." If you have a poisonous or toxic plant in your garden, at least one chicken is guaranteed to eat it. If you have predators in your area, one of them will eventually kill one of your chickens. Your job is to reduce the frequency of these incidents.

It's better to be safe than sorry, so avoid the following garden plants that could kill your chickens:

Azalea	Bulbs (most types of bulbs)	Buttercup
Castor Bean	Clematis	Climbing lily
Corn Cockle	Foxglove	Henbane
Honeysuckle	Iris	Lily of the Valley
Lobelia	Lupine	Periwinkle
Sweet Pea	Ragwort	Rhododendron
St. John's Wort	Trumpet Vine	Vetch
Yew (all parts of the tree)		

Some plants are only toxic in large quantities, but many of them spread prolifically, and **toxins are cumulative**. This gives your chickens plenty of unfortunate opportunity to eat large quantities - or to eat small quantities regularly. These plants include:

Acorns
Bracken fern
Holly
Rhubarb

Nightshades deserve a special mention here. As well as 'deadly nightshade' (the name is a bit of a giveaway), there are over two thousand other varieties of nightshade. These include common plants like eggplant/aubergine, tomatoes, potatoes and peppers/capsicum, tamarillo, gooseberry, blueberry, and chili. All nightshades contain alkaloids, which cause loss of appetite, weak heart, and breathing troubles in chickens.

Predators:

No matter where you live, you'll have local predators. Depending on where you live, these can range from eagles and bears, to snakes and raccoons. The first step is to identify your local predators; only then can you work out how to protect your flock. In many cases, you'll already know the predators in your area. If you live near to bears or alligators, I'd be astonished if you didn't already know about their presence!

If your chickens are already going missing or are being killed, you need to work out what's preying on them. You can do this by observation (seeing or filming the attack) or deduction (looking at the evidence). Security cameras are a simple way to keep an eye on your flock, and they don't have to cost the earth. If your coop is near a power supply, old smartphones with security camera apps are an inexpensive way to monitor predators.

If your adult chickens are missing and there's no sign of what happened, you're probably looking at something dog-like, for example, a coyote, wolf, or fox, or a large flying predator like a hawk, eagle or owl. Hawks and eagles tend to feed during the day, while owls attack at night. Chicks missing without a sign, or with only a few feathers left behind, are likely to have been taken by a snake, rat, raccoon, or cat.

Weasels often kill chickens and eat only the internal organs or try to pull intestines out through the victim's vent; while headless bodies could be a result of hawks or owls. If you find headless chickens near the fence, it's probably a raccoon; they sometimes pull a chicken's head through the wire but can't get the rest of the chicken through, so they just eat the head. If you find your birds wounded, but not dead, there are several possibilities. If the chickens are covered in bites, it might be a dog. Bites on breasts or legs point to an opossum, while bites on the hocks could be rats. Missing eggs could be a wide range of predators, from skunks and snakes to quolls and Tasmanian devils. If you sprinkle fine sand or talc around your coop, the tracks might give you some indication of what you're dealing with. If you're still stumped, local farmers are the best source of advice for identifying what's attacking your chickens, and how you might be able to handle them.

You can stop predators by improving the enclosure's defenses, using a guard animal, or by exterminating the predators yourself. In most cases, a multi-pronged approach works best. We discussed the basics of security and fencing in Chapter 3. If predators are getting through your current fencing, upgrading may help. Electric fences that stun predators are one of the most effective methods to protect a flock.

When you install an electric fence, it's tempting to "turn it up" to kill predators. This is counter-productive. If a predator just gets a painful jolt from the fence, it learns to stay away from the fence. If instead, the shock kills it, a new predator will move into the vacant territory soon enough. Low-power fences are also less dangerous to you, your children, your pets, and your chickens.

A rooster is the obvious guardian for a flock, but roosters also sleep deeply at night. A properly trained guard dog can live with the flock, protect the chickens, deter predators, and raise the alarm. When it comes to choosing a dog to protect your chickens, you need to choose a protective, easy-to-train breed, that isn't likely to attack your chickens. Selecting and training a guard dog is beyond the scope of this book, but no matter what breed you choose - don't forget to get your chickens used to the dog. If they start attacking their guard, it will only complicate matters.

If it's legal in your area, killing or trapping persistent predators is a valid strategy. Some considerations to make are:

Is the predator a protected species? What method do you want to use? Is it safe and legal to do so?

Before you go any further, look up which species are protected in your area. Many predators, particularly birds of prey, are protected species. Before you can trap a predator, you need to know what it is, choose a trap, choose where to put the trap, and bait the trap. There are two basic types of traps: traps that keep trapped creatures alive, and traps that kill them. Live traps are a humane way to get rid of predators, as long as you check them daily. Leaving trapped or injured animals to starve to death is cruel and unnecessary.

If you're planning to set your trap near your chickens, make sure they're locked in their coop (you don't want to inadvertently catch them instead of the predator) and have a plan for what to do once you've trapped your target. When you place the trap, avoid wearing strong scents (perfume, cologne, deodorant, scented soap) as that may scare the predator away. Whatever you do, check your traps regularly and make sure you're wearing appropriate equipment to protect yourself from whatever you've trapped. If you're using a live trap, covering it with a blanket as you approach may help to calm the animal. Poison bait stations can help with some predators, particularly rats, mice, and possums (where they're not protected), but they're not ideal. The problem with poison is twofold: first, your chickens could eat it; and second, your chickens could eat the poisoned corpse. Neither will have a happy ending. If you use poison to control predators, make sure your chickens can't access the bait and remove dead animals promptly before your chickens decide that the poisoned corpse looks like a nutritious dinner!

Depending on the predator, your competence, and your local laws, shooting may be effective for ridding certain predators. If you live in a place where this is legal, it's worth considering for larger predators. Of course, you'll need to comply with local gun laws and gun-safety rules.

As I mentioned in Chapter 5, foraging chickens will eat almost anything! Ticks, slugs, snails, spiders, worms, moths, flies, ants, termites, cockroaches, mosquitoes, and even small snakes and frogs are fair game for a foraging chicken. Chickens have even been known to de-flea cats and dogs. While they don't eat moles, chicken owners with mole problems report that moles often move out when they have to share their worms with the chickens.

Unless you desire particular bugs in your garden, there's no down-side to this: free feed and extra protein for your chickens, and fewer pests/more eggs for you.

One of the challenges of the fact that chickens are indiscriminate omnivores is that they sometimes eat other chickens. Chicken cannibalism has several causes. As you already know, pecking is a normal way to establish and maintain the pecking order. This can lead to feather plucking. The resulting bleeding can trigger all the chickens to "peck the red bit," killing the victim. Cannibalism results. Cannibalism can happen in any flock; however, it's less common in small flocks, stable flocks with fewer new chickens, and flocks that have lots of space to roam. For reasons unknown to me, cannibalism is more common in breeds that lay brown-shelled eggs, than those that lay white-shelled eggs.

Fortunately, it's quite easy to prevent cannibalism - by considering these factors below.

At a high level, they each come down to stress. A relaxed, comfortable, stable, happy flock is unlikely to resort to cannibalism.

Space - As I've said several times, overcrowding can lead to stress. Stress causes a wide range of problems, cannibalism being one of them. Make sure your chickens have enough space in all areas - including around feeders and waterers.

Temperature - Like us, chickens like to be warm - but not too warm. Make sure they have enough cool water and ventilation. For chicks in a brooder, make sure they have a corner to get away from the heat lamp if they're too hot.

Light - Likewise, hens need light to produce eggs, but too much light will cause stress. If you have white artificial lights in the coop, don't use more than 40W, and never leave them on for more than sixteen hours a day. If you need to leave heat lamps on continuously, use red or infrared lamps, not white ones.

Nutrition - Chickens are very good at finding foods that contain nutrients they're missing. It's no surprise that cannibalism has been linked with protein, sodium, and phosphorous deficiencies. Methionine deficiency can cause feather plucking, while high-energy, low-fiber diets can make chickens aggressive. When chickens preen, they use oil from the preen gland near their tail. The oil is salty. If the chickens are low on salt, they may start overusing their gland, leading to broken feathers and starting the pecking-bleeding-cannibalism cycle. If you use an appropriate, high-quality feed for the age and type of chicken, you shouldn't have issues.

Natural behavior and boredom - Chickens' natural behavior is to spend most of the day scratching, pecking, and foraging for food. If they can't do this, they sometimes redirect the scratching and pecking towards their flock mates, with a predictable outcome. Even if you don't let your chickens forage, provide something to encourage that behavior. Scratch, straw, grass clippings, and mash all force chickens to scratch, peck, and hunt for food. If you do this, don't forget to clean up regularly, otherwise the leftover food will attract pests. Giving them something to play with, for example, hanging lettuce leaves or herbs around the coop, helps to reduce boredom.

Removal of injured and dead birds - Any blood will tempt chickens to peck. This means that any bleeding injury can lead to pecking. Make sure there are no sharp wires, protruding nails or similar that could injure your birds. Prevent injuries, and you can avoid pecking. If any chickens are injured or killed, remove them immediately, along with any cannibalistic chickens. You don't want them to get in the habit of killing and eating their flock members.

Flock size - In the wild, chickens live in flocks of about fifteen. The flock is small enough that they all know each other. When you keep them in a flock of over thirty, they can't recognize everyone else in the flock. This makes it impossible to keep track of the pecking order, and the social order breaks down.

Mingling chickens of different age, breed, and color - Mingling flocks of completely different birds increases the chances of cannibalism. If you want to keep a mixture of chickens of different breeds, colors, or sizes, raise them together from when they are young, to encourage a stable pecking order. Some breeds are more dominant than others; older birds are more dominant than younger ones; larger birds are more dominant than smaller ones. Chickens' natural curiosity will make them peck unfamiliar features. If your chickens have never seen chickens with feathered feet, or crests, when you introduce chickens with those features, your chickens are likely to start pecking at their new flock mates.

You already spend time watching your chickens. Make a point of watching for feather damage that could indicate pecking. One or two broken feathers isn't a problem, but it's worth keeping an eye on; one or more large bare patches is a problem; and bare patches with broken skin is a serious problem.

If you notice a problem, remove the aggressive chicken (or chickens) and any injured birds. Care for the injured birds and work through the above list of cannibalism causes. Look for things you can do to reduce stress or distract the rest of the flock.

As a last resort, you can try chicken goggles. In the past, beak trimming was recommended, but it's now rightly illegal in several countries.

Managing change - Chickens like stability. Sudden changes lead to stress, so if you need to change something, do it in small steps. If you need to move them to a different coop, move the portable equipment from the old coop as well.

Inadequate nesting boxes – As I explained in Chapter 6, hens like to lay eggs in a dark, secure, comfortable place. In a well-designed and well-managed coop, this will be the nesting boxes. There is a reason they're more comfortable in the dark. When they lay an egg, the inside of the vent is exposed. It's pink, so any chickens that see it will be drawn to peck it. Some outbreaks of chicken cannibalism have started during egg-laying in poorly-designed nesting boxes.

Egg Cannibalism

Many of us raise chickens for fresh eggs. And rightly so - they're delicious. Unfortunately, many chickens agree. When they learn how good eggs taste, it's hard to blame them for eating their own eggs. It's also difficult to stop them. Feeding eggs to your chickens as a treat makes sense at a practical level, but it can also teach them that eggs are a tasty source of food. To avoid this, only feed them cooked eggs. Scrambled or boiled eggs are easy to make, and they look and taste nothing like raw eggs. The primary reason chickens might eat their eggs is a lack of protein. If they're not getting enough protein from their feed, they can turn to eggs as a supplement. For adult chickens, check that their feed is at least 16% protein, and supplement it with high-protein treats like sunflower seeds.

If the eggshells are thin, then the eggs may break easily, prompting the chicken to eat it. In this case, oyster shells will help to increase your hens' calcium level, allowing them to make stronger eggs – as mentioned previously. If the basics are covered, and your hens have enough protein and calcium, they may just have a taste for eggs. In this case, it's time to get creative. As well as collecting eggs frequently, so your chickens have less chance to eat them, you can use decoys and tricks to teach them that eggs aren't good food.

Put a wooden egg or golf ball in the nest. She won't be able to break into it and may give up. Alternatively, make a small hole at each end of a fresh egg, blow the contents out, fill it with mustard, and place it in her nesting box. Most chickens absolutely detest mustard, so it might put her off eating eggs. If nothing helps, you can try changing the design of your nesting boxes. Cushioned nesting boxes allow the egg to drop into a padded box where the chickens can't get to it, while in slanted nesting boxes roll away so the chickens can't find them.

Chapter 9 – Optimal Chicken Health & Simple Treatments

Every day, you should watch your chickens for a while to get used to their normal behavior and note any changes that could signal a health problem. Whenever you handle them, or at least once a week, check each of your chickens for any signs of ill health, as described in Chapter 4. I find that when I clean the coop, it is a good time to give them a once-over. A normal, happy, healthy chicken is bright-eyed, active, alert, and curious. It breathes easily, interacts with other chickens, and forages for food.

All being well, you'll quickly become familiar with how a healthy chicken looks and behaves. That's a useful reference for identifying an unhealthy chicken - it's one that doesn't look and act like the healthy ones. One problem with chickens is that they're very good at hiding health problems. When you're getting started, if you're in any doubt at all, take them to the vet.

As you become more familiar with your chickens, you have more wiggle room for either waiting or trying to heal them yourself. A sick chicken will often stand out from the flock because they'll behave differently from the healthy birds.

Behavioral signs of assorted health problems are:

Hiding	Weight loss, or changes in appetite	Weakness or lethargy
Fluffed-up feathers	Falling over	Hunched over posture with tail down
Trailing wings	Changes in laying behavior	Drinking more water than usual

| Lack of curiosity | Other behavioural changes | |

General physical signs of illness are:

Dull eyes	Losing feathers (except when molting)	Crop feels squishy or rigid
Abdomen feels rigid, swollen, squishy or hot	Limping or difficulty walking	Changes in droppings
Pale comb and/or wattles	Feathers around the vent matted or dirty	

If chickens have respiratory diseases (or gapeworm), they'll be sneezing, panting or gasping, and may have discharge running from their eyes and nose.

You now know how to check whether your chickens are healthy or not. Next, you'll learn what could be wrong with them and more importantly, what you can do about it.

Molting can be alarming if you haven't seen it before, but it's nothing to worry about. Once a year, usually in the autumn/fall, your chickens will lose their feathers and grow new ones. The process generally takes around three months. Molting chickens look ragged and bare, and usually stop laying eggs. You can't do anything except wait.

Several types of **mites and blood-sucking parasites** affect chickens. The precise signs vary depending on the type of mite. Some burrow under scales, while others hide in the coop and bite at night. Roost or red mites look like tiny brown or red spots. They're often squashed on the outside of the eggs, or hiding under the roosting perches. If you run a paper towel under an infested roosting perch, you'll find red smears of squashed mites on the towel. Mite droppings, which look like piles of cigarette ash, are another good way to detect them. Chickens will refuse to lay in mite-infested nesting boxes, and untreated roost mites can kill your chickens.

Chickens suffering from **roost mites** will scratch a lot. You may see bare patches of skin, ruffled feathers, reduced laying, and diarrhea. Affected chickens will probably be less active than usual, and may be unwilling to go back in the coop at night. Mites and lice like dark, dirty coops. To prevent mites, keep the coop clean and make sure all new arrivals are mite-free before introducing them to the flock. Working diatomaceous earth into the coop surfaces when cleaning can help to prevent mites and lice, but make sure you use protective equipment to avoid dust inhalation. Sprinkling dried pennyworth and peppermint can help to repel mites, too.

To treat an infestation of mites and lice, you need to treat the coop and the chickens separately. Permethrin, a broad-spectrum insecticide, is an effective way to treat a bad mite infestation in a coop, and diatomaceous earth can treat your chickens. If you give your birds a sandpit full of sand mixed with diatomaceous earth, they'll cheerfully treat themselves. You'll also need to thoroughly clean the coop and everything in it (including the chickens), and burn and replace the bedding - just spreading permethrin isn't enough.

Burrowing mites are quite common. They burrow under chickens' leg scales, which is as uncomfortable as it sounds. If your chicken has burrowing mites, the scales will be visibly raised. While it's tempting, don't pull any scales off - you'll make things worse. Apply Vaseline (petroleum jelly) regularly to soften the scales and suffocate the mites. Once a week, dip the legs in surgical spirit before you apply Vaseline.

Parasitic worms such as tapeworm, roundworm, and gapeworm can kill chickens; and prevention is better than cure. Good hygiene and regular worming are the best way to prevent worms. You can start worming your chickens when you move them outdoors at about eight to ten weeks old. Any off-the-shelf worm treatment should be fine, as long as you follow the instructions. The main worms that affect chickens are hairworm, tapeworm, and roundworm, which affect the digestive system; and gapeworm, which affects the trachea and lungs.

Signs of **worm infestation** include listlessness (lacking in energy), weight loss, appetite changes, lower egg production, pale combs, breathing difficulties, irritation around the vent, vomiting, and whiteness in the droppings. Gapeworm can also cause sneezing and discharge around the eyes and nostrils, which you could easily mistake for a respiratory disease. If your hens have a serious infestation, you might even find worms in their eggs. If you suspect worms, some people say pumpkin, chicken seeds, apple cider vinegar (1 tablespoon per gallon), or garlic cloves in water will help. While they probably won't hurt, I normally just go with medication. The treatment needs to match the type of worm, so send a dropping sample to your vet. They'll be able to identify the worm type and recommend an appropriate treatment. Chapter 11 will discuss this in more detail.

Chickens don't catch colds. If your chickens show signs that would, in humans, indicate a cold, something else is wrong. These signs could include sneezing, runny eyes and noses, and rattled breathing. Poor ventilation, ammonia, and dust in the coop increase the likelihood of **respiratory diseases**. Most respiratory diseases in chickens are caused by viruses, not bacteria. This means that antibiotics probably won't help. Because there are so many possible respiratory diseases, some of which may even be dangerous to humans, you should really see a vet for a proper diagnosis and appropriate treatment.

Frostbite is the same in chickens as in humans. Exposed, sensitive parts can freeze. If you live in a particularly cold area, a heated coop will reduce the likelihood of any frostbite. If it's only an occasional problem, coating chickens' combs and wattles in Vaseline (petroleum jelly), or knitting them little woolly hats can reduce frostbite.

Frostbitten combs and wattles look purple rather than a healthy red, and might feel cold and rigid. A day later, you may notice fluid-filled blisters, and several days later, the tissue may turn black. Frostbitten feet can cause chickens to limp. Always take a frostbitten chicken somewhere warm before you try to treat them. Gradually warm the affected area with lukewarm water, or flannels soaked in lukewarm water (100-101F). Don't rub them though - it'll hurt, and could cause more damage. Contact a vet for advice, painkillers, and anti-inflammatory medication. If the flesh turns black, don't remove it, and don't burst blisters. If the area becomes swollen and inflamed, it may be infected.

As with humans, diarrhea can be a sign of lots of different chicken problems, ranging from parasites to poisoning. As with most chicken health problems, a clean coop and good nutrition go a long way to preventing the most common causes of diarrhea. If any of your birds have diarrhea, you'll notice it under the roost when you check the coop in the morning. You can find out which bird it is by checking the feathers around the vent or looking for stained eggs. When a chicken has diarrhea, immediately check the feed isn't moldy, the water in the waterers is clean and fresh, and that there are no indications of worms or other illnesses.

When you find the affected hen, check for *vent prolapse*, which will appear like a large pink bulge sticking out of the vent. This is manageable, but it can cause diarrhea. If the other chickens start pecking it, things will go downhill fast. **Vent prolapse** is also known as a blowout. It can be caused by hens laying eggs that are too large, by a calcium and magnesium deficiency, being over/underweight, or an abdominal/oviduct infection. Early signs of prolapse can include signs of distress, blood on the eggs, listlessness, low egg production, or bullying from the rest of the flock.

When you find a vent prolapse, separate the hen and keep her somewhere dark and quiet. The lack of light will stop or reduce laying. Clean the exposed tissue gently with warm water and a little bit of mild antiseptic, like iodine. Once it's clean, lubricate it (water-based lubricant & hemorrhoid cream both work well) and gently push it back inside. If the protruding tissue was cut or abraded, talk to your vet about giving the hen antibiotics to prevent internal infection. While she's recovering, keep her separated from the flock, give her extra vitamins, magnesium, and calcium, and make sure she doesn't get enough sun to trigger egg-laying.

Chickens store foraged food in their crop, which is a small pouch at the end of their esophagus, so they can digest it later. An **impacted crop** is a blocked crop. It's dangerous because an affected chicken won't be able to digest any food. The most common cause of impacted crop is an over-optimistic chicken trying to store something indigestible like straw, sand, wood, or plastic. These kind of things build up, blocking the crop. Diseases or parasites that restrict gut movement are the other main cause of impacted crop. This includes diseases like Marek's disease, lead poisoning, worms, or physical damage to the digestive system. The blockage is sometimes visible, but sometimes it goes the other way and sticks into the gizzard where you can't see it.

Treat **impacted crop** by feeding the chicken grit, and commercial mash/crumbs. For drinking, add a tablespoon of vinegar to each gallon of water. If it doesn't start to improve in a few days, consult your local vet. If the crop doesn't empty completely, it's a cozy place for a fungus called Candida to grow. When this happens, we call it sour crop, it makes the crop wall thicken, and the crop dilate.

First thing in the morning, the crop should be flat. If it's still full and squishy, it's probably sour crop. You might also notice a sour smell on the chicken's breath, white patches in their mouth, and diarrhea. All sorts of things, including impacted crop, infection, worms, and antibiotics, can lead to sour crop. If you catch it early, isolate the chicken and gently massage the crop from top to bottom every few hours to try to make the contents move on towards the gut. Don't feed or give water to them for the first twelve hours. After twelve hours, you can give them water, but no food. After another twelve hours, if the crop is flat, start her on small amounts of scrambled eggs or yogurt with mash. Three or four small meals a day, plus as much water as necessary, will be enough.

If fluid is leaking from the chicken's beak, it means that the **crop is overflowing**. Ideally, consult a vet. If you can't or don't want to, you'll need to massage the fluid out of her crop. This isn't difficult, but if you do it wrong, the chicken can inhale the fluid. Sit down, wrap the chicken in a towel, lean her over your knees with her head towards the ground, and massage her crop from bottom to top until the fluid comes out. Repeat this three or four times, no more than four times a day, for fifteen or twenty seconds each time. Hold the chicken upright between attempts. If this doesn't work, you should definitely consult a vet for anti-fungal medication.

You'll definitely notice if you have a chicken with a twisted neck, also known as **wry neck, or stargazing.** The chicken's neck will be twisted so that they're looking behind them or up at the sky, and they'll have trouble standing, eating, and drinking. It's most common in chicks. While it can be a sign of a head injury, genetic anomaly, or Marek's disease, it's usually caused by a vitamin E deficiency. To treat it, remove the affected chick, but keep them near the rest of the flock or give them a toy for company. Give them vitamin E and selenium supplements. The main treatment is vitamin E, but the selenium helps with absorption. You'll need to help them eat and drink. When the neck posture improves, you can return them to the rest of the flock. Continue with the supplementation for at least two weeks.

Fatty liver hemorrhagic syndrome (FLHS) is the major cause of mortality in caged hens. Chickens with FLHS have extra fat in their liver and abdomen, resulting in an enlarged liver prone to bleeding. When a hen with FLHS is straining to lay an egg, the liver bursts and the hen bleeds out. While chickens with FLHS are often overweight and sometimes have pale combs, in most cases, there are no obvious signs prior to sudden death. This makes prevention the only option. In 2019, a study showed that 74% of caged hens died from FLHS, versus less than 5% of cage-free or free-range hens. To reduce the chances of FLHS, let your hens free-range and forage, and don't overfeed them.

Splayed or spraddle leg is a common leg problem in chicks and other birds. You'll definitely notice it: it looks like the chick's doing the splits, and they won't be able to walk. It can be congenital, or can develop later if the broodery floor is too slippery. If it was congenital, it suggests that the parents were nutritionally deficient. This often happens when you feed layers pellets to breeding chickens, for example. If it wasn't congenital, you can prevent it from developing in the first place: don't use newspaper or any other slippery material to line the brooder. Paper towels or non-slip matting are effective, affordable, non-slippery substitutes.

Fortunately, splayed leg is easy to fix if you notice it early. In essence, you need to remove the chick from the flock and tie the legs together with "cuffs." Two easy options for cuffs are an elastic band passed through a straw, or vet-wrap cuffs with a thin strip around each leg, then one strip to join them. No matter which method you choose, make sure the cuffs aren't too tight, but still tight enough that they won't slip off.

Bumblefoot is a foot problem caused by constant, uneven pressure on the bottom of the foot, similar to how humans develop bedsores. The skin breaks down, bacteria get in, and the infection starts. At first, all you'll see is shiny pink swelling on the sole of the foot, and sometimes flaking skin. As the infection progresses, you'll see more swelling, callouses, and then a large sore. At this stage, the chicken will be limping. If you ignore it, eventually, you'll start to see a plug of dead tissue or a scab in the middle of the sore, and the chicken won't be able to walk. Leave it long enough, and the infection will spread through the chicken's body, potentially killing them.

If you catch it early enough, soaking the affected foot in a solution of Epsom salts in warm water can help. Alternatively, use a solution of iodine or chlorohexidine. If it's more severe, contact your vet. To prevent bumblefoot, don't put the roosting perches too high and make sure the coop and bedding are clean and free of splinters. If your chickens frequently get bumblefoot, sometimes using sand rather than shavings or straw as bedding, helps.

A hen who can't lay is **egg-bound**. She'll probably be sitting on the ground, feathers all puffed up, tired from trying to lay her egg. This is an urgent problem: if she can't lay it within forty-eight hours, she will die. Rough handling before she's laid her egg can sometimes break the egg inside the hen, leading to egg-binding, but there are other causes. The only thing you can do is keep her warm and comfortable. Put her in a warm cage with a pan of water underneath for moist heat, a heat lamp overhead to keep the temperature between 90 and 102F, and plenty of water to drink.

Fowl or avian pox is caused by a contagious virus. Chickens can catch it through broken skin, biting insects, other infected birds, or contaminated surfaces. It appears as white spots on the skin, sores and scabs on combs and wattles, and ulcers in the mouth and throat. You'll also notice a loss of appetite and decreased egg production. Fighting roosters are more prone to catch fowl pox because of broken skin. As always, prevention is better than cure: vaccinate your birds before they catch it. Once they've got it, there's no treatment, only supportive care. If fowl pox leads to a secondary bacterial infection, that can often be treated with antibiotics, but that won't help with the virus.

Separate the affected birds, keep them in a warm, dry coop and feed them soft food. Most chickens survive fowl pox.

No matter how well you look after your chickens, one or two will eventually get ill. It's worth planning in advance how you're going to deal with it and where you're going to quarantine sick chickens. If one of your chickens is ill, it doesn't matter what's wrong with them: remove them from the flock, quarantine them in an isolation pen, and thoroughly clean the coop, run, and all associated equipment. Until you know for sure that it's not contagious, you need to assume that it is, and protect the rest of your flock. Whenever you put a chicken in quarantine, monitor the rest of the flock closely in case any of the others may be affected by the same problem.

While a chicken is in quarantine, make sure they have plenty of clean water and the feed that they're used to. If they're not eating or drinking, you can hand-feed them a liquid diet with a spoon, dripper, or syringe. Don't give them medication unless you know what's wrong with them – randomized medicine can make things much, much worse. This includes antibiotics. If you feed a chicken antibiotics when the problem isn't a bacterial infection, it actually increases all your chickens' chances of having antibiotic-resistant bacterial infections in the future.

In many cases, sick chickens will recover after a few days. In that case, keep them isolated for a few additional days to be sure they've completely recovered, then let them out to rejoin the flock. When you reintroduce a recovered chicken to the flock, introduce them slowly as if they were a complete stranger. This reduces stress and avoids violence. When the sick bird has returned to the main flock, don't forget to thoroughly disinfect the isolation pen.

Vaccinating your chickens is an effective way to prevent or reduce certain diseases, but it's not a substitute for proper care and hygiene. As a backyard chicken keeper, vaccinating your chickens presents challenges, as many suppliers only supply vaccines in batches of 500 or 1000. Chickens bought from commercial breeders are normally vaccinated, but buying vaccines for small numbers of chicks can be prohibitively expensive. To complicate things, most vaccines only work on chicks during their first few weeks of life.

You'll need to weigh up the likelihood and prevalence of chicken diseases in your area against the cost and the likelihood that your chickens will be exposed to each disease. If you have a mixed flock of vaccinated and unvaccinated chickens, consider keeping them separate, especially when they're young. Vaccinated chickens can carry and spread diseases like Marek's disease to unvaccinated birds.

We've touched on stress a few times in previous chapters, so you already know some of the causes, and that it can lead to cannibalism. Here I'll focus on the other effects and signs of stress. In every instance, the solution is to identify and reduce the source of stress. When chickens encounter a source of stress, their reactions go through three stages: alarm, adaption, and exhaustion. We often call the "alarm" stage the "fight, flight or freeze" response. Most chickens tend strongly towards flight. In this stage, the brain releases adrenaline into the system. The adrenaline triggers cortisol, which releases glucose to the blood, giving the chicken energy to escape. As the chicken adapts, the levels of adrenaline and cortisol should drop. Exhaustion occurs when a chicken doesn't recover from the stressor. It uses up its energy reserves and dies.

As a chicken keeper, it's your job to reduce sources of stress and encourage adaption to the unavoidable stressors. When chickens are threatened by a change such as accommodation or feed, they usually adapt quickly once they work out that whatever's happening to them isn't actually a threat.

Sources of stress can be summarized into several broad categories:

Environmental (temperature, coop design, and lighting);
Health and nutrition;
Physical (physical handling, transport);
Physiological (injuries);
Psychological (predators, loud noises); and
Social (new chickens in the flock, bullying, pecking order issues).

If it's not immediately obvious what's causing stress, start by looking for anything that's changed and go from there.

Nutritional deficiencies can lead to a truly astounding range of effects, none of which are healthy. Listless chickens may not be getting enough carbohydrates, protein, and magnesium, while abnormal feather growth could be due to any of several nutrients. Diets lacking in certain amino acids, niacin, folic acid, zinc, or cobalamin can make feathers grow strangely. If the feathers are blackened, vitamin D deficiency is a likely culprit, while if they're white, your chickens are probably low on lysine. If they're less red than usual, check your chickens are getting enough copper and iron.

With chicks, if their feathers are growing curled up inside their follicles (known as "clubbed down"), consider riboflavin (vitamin B2) deficiency. Riboflavin and pantothenic acid (vitamin B3) deficiencies are also associated with neurological disorders in chicks, including curled toe paralysis. This paralyzes the chicks' toes, forcing them to rest on their hocks. If your chickens have recurring skin irritations and inflammation, it could be niacin, biotin, or pantothenic acid deficiencies. If they get lesions on the bottom of their feet or skin irritation around their eyes, biotin supplements can help.

Crazy chick disease is easy to diagnose: two or three-week-old chicks start falling over and develop twisted neck syndrome. This is caused by a lack of vitamin E. Insufficient vitamin A can lead to bone weakness and deformation, but it's not quite that simple. Chickens also need vitamin

D, calcium, and phosphorous to support healthy bone development. If the ratio is wrong or the quantities are insufficient, they can develop cage layer disease. These chickens have brittle bones and a particularly fragile rib cage. Reduced egg production in hens can be caused by insufficient vitamin D, magnesium, manganese, potassium, sodium, or chloride; while thin eggshells are a giveaway that the hen's not getting enough vitamin D, folic acid, magnesium or manganese.

As with so many health problems, prevention is better than cure. If you feed your chickens with an appropriate good quality pellet for their age and type, you'll avoid the majority of nutritional problems. For animals that have lived with us for so long, there are still some amazing myths still going around about keeping chickens. There is enough chicken research and actual facts that you don't need to resort to myths.

Chapter 10 – Chicken Keeping Myths Destroyed

Myth 1: Chickens are dirty, smelly animals

Any animal that's not properly cared for will always smell. If you keep your coop clean and compost the droppings, neither your chickens nor your coop will smell.

An average healthy chicken produces about 1.5 ounces of droppings a day. Compared to the average dog which produces about twelve ounces, you'll have far fewer chicken droppings to deal with! If your chickens' smell, it's entirely on you. Keep the coop clean, feed them a healthy diet, give them somewhere for dust baths, don't overcrowd your coop, and you shouldn't have any problems with smelly chickens.

Myth 2: Chickens carry disease

This is closely related to myth 1. If you neglect your chickens, just like any animal, they can carry disease. Chickens eat bugs like ticks, that when alive, can transmit diseases to humans. While you can catch salmonella from chicken droppings, you can avoid it with common-sense precautions. Wash your hands when you've finished handling your chickens, and you're no more likely to catch a disease from your well-cared-for chickens than from any other pet.

Concerning the question, "Does bird flu spread easily from birds to humans?" the World Health Organization website says:

"No. Despite the extension and duration of the outbreaks in animals presenting vast opportunities for animal to human exposure (particularly in areas where backyard flocks are common) - the number of human H5N1 avian influenza cases remains very small."

Similarly, the 2006 Grain Report states: *"When it comes to bird flu, diverse small-scale poultry is the solution, not the problem."*

Myth 3: Chickens attract pests and predators

It's a sad fact, but no matter whether you live in an urban or rural area, you've almost certainly already got pests and predators in your area. This myth exists because you'll become more aware of them when you start keeping chickens, but that's not because they suddenly appeared out of nowhere. The key to reducing pests and predators' interest in your chickens is to keep the chickens secure and the area clean. Store feed in predator-proof containers, and secure feeders, waterers, and chickens at night. If the predators and pests find no food, they may lose interest. The chickens can also deal with any smaller pests themselves.

Myth 4: Chickens are noisy

This is subjective. What do you mean by noisy? And by chickens, do you mean hens or roosters?

We measure noise levels in decibels. The noise of a clucking chicken is 60 to 70 decibels, while a crowing rooster is about 90 decibels.

Since that probably doesn't mean much to you, here are some other noise levels for comparison:

- Human conversation: 50-65 decibels
- Flushing toilet or vacuum cleaner: 70 decibels
- Motorcycle: 80 decibels
- Barking dog: 90 decibels
- Crickets: 80-100 decibels
- Frog: 90-120 decibels
- Crying baby: 100-110 decibels
- Cicadas: 100-120 decibels
- Chainsaw: 100-120 decibels

So, an average hen is quieter than crickets, cicadas, dogs, and frogs, and only slightly louder than you having a conversation. Crowing roosters, on the other hand, are undeniably noisy - at about the same level as a barking dog.

Myth 5: You need a rooster to lay eggs

If you consider an egg as a chicken's period, it's obvious why this myth makes no sense.

When a hen gets enough light, her body will release an egg from her ovaries. Male chickens' only role with regard to eggs is to fertilize them. Hens in flocks with no roosters will still lay eggs; they'll just never hatch. But they'll still taste great!

Myth 6: Hens lays an egg each day

Nope. Most hens lay four or five eggs a week, but it depends on their breed, age, health, and on environmental conditions. When they're molting, sick, stressed, or kept in the dark, they'll lay fewer eggs. Chapter 6 goes through some ways to increase your egg production, but it's quite rare to actually collect an egg every day.

Myth 7: Brown eggs are more nutritious than white eggs

Definitely not. A hen's diet determines the nutritional content of an egg, and the hen's breed determines the color of the shell. A small study in 2016 found that "... the best egg in terms of the nutritional value was from family-type chickens living in their natural environment."

A free-ranging foraging hen eats a more varied diet and produces an egg with lower cholesterol and saturated fat, as well as more Vitamin A and E. In addition, free-range eggs contain more beta-carotene and omega-3 oil than eggs from a hen which survives solely on commercial corn or grain-based feed.

Myth 8: Backyard chickens will reduce the value of property in my area

While you might not think this, your neighbors might. It's not unreasonable, from their perspective. Here are some facts that might help you to calm them down. In the years leading up to 2014 in the USA, there was no documented case of backyard chickens lowering the property value of the neighborhood. In the same year, neighborhoods that decided to allow backyard chickens saw no decrease in property values. If your neighbors are concerned, talk to them and take their concerns seriously.

Sometimes fresh eggs can be a good enough bribe.

Myth 9: You can tell the sex of an unhatched chicken

In short, you can't. Believe me. If it was possible, commercial hatcheries would definitely do it that way rather than culling day-old male chicks. In 2002, Horiuchi and Towa Sangyo filed a patent for a device to determine the sex of a fertilized egg; it was abandoned in 2004. In 2018, a German company developed a way to determine the sex of an unhatched egg by using a laser to burn a hole in the egg, extracting a fluid sample, and testing it for particular hormones. As yet, it's not in commercial use, and it's unlikely to be cost-effective for backyard chicken owners. Some used to believe that the shape of the egg or the size of the air sac was related to the sex of the chicken. While that would make life much easier, unfortunately, the two variables completely unrelated.

Myth 10: Chickens are hard to care for

Since you've made it this far, you already know that caring for chickens is straightforward once you have the right knowledge. If you have half an hour each day, plus a few hours a couple of times a year, you have the time and knowledge to keep chickens!

Chapter 11 – Flock Maintenance & Butchering Broilers

In this chapter, you'll find a quick summary of exactly what you'll need to do daily, weekly, monthly, and a few times each year to care for your resident chickens.

Daily Tasks

You'll need to spend just fifteen or twenty minutes a day on your daily tasks.

Let the chickens out of the coop in the morning, make sure they've got enough food and water for the day, clean up the worst of the droppings under the roost, and collect the eggs. Don't forget to check that the droppings look more-or-less the same as usual, and check there's no blood on the eggs. Any abnormalities can indicate a health problem.

Sometime during the day, check again for eggs and spend a few minutes watching and interacting with the flock. That last bit isn't compulsory, but it helps you catch any problems early - and it's fun!

In the evening, get them back into the coop, lock the door, secure the food and water, and clean up any scratch or other food on the ground. That's all for the daily tasks.

Weekly Tasks

Your main weekly chore is to clean the coop and run, including changing the bedding and disinfecting the feeders and waterers. If it's hot, or your flock is particularly messy, you might need to clean out the feeders and waterers twice a week.

At the same time, give each of your chickens a proper once-over to check for any developing health problems. You can do this more than once a week, but make sure you do it at least once a week. Once you get your system down, this shouldn't take more than an hour a week.

A Few Times a Year

At least every few months, or when you notice it's getting smelly, deep clean the coop. This is elaborated on in just a second. This should only take a few hours. While you're at it, don't forget to check for (and fix) any developing maintenance problems.

Changing Seasons

As seasons change, you'll need to prepare the coop for the new season. As winter approaches, add extra bedding and double-check that the coop is watertight. If you live somewhere where it freezes in winter, install heaters in your coop and waterers. Make sure they're all properly secured and are unlikely to start fires or burn your chickens. As spring approaches and it warms up, you can clean and pack away the winter gear, ready for next year.

Cleaning Your Coop

You'll need to clean your feeders and waterers daily, and your coop and run at least weekly. Ideally, clean your feeders and waterers daily, but you might be able to get away with every second day. I give mine a quick clean, then stick them in the dishwasher. If you're not comfortable putting chicken equipment anywhere near your dishes, hot soapy water will do the job just fine. You need to clean your coop at least weekly. If the weather is particularly hot or your chickens are inside more than usual, you might need to increase to twice a week. The smell of ammonia is a good guide: if you can smell it in and around the coop, it's time to clean it.

Some chickens insist on sleeping in the nesting boxes. If you have any like this, you'll need to clean their nesting boxes daily. Otherwise, the droppings will start to build up.

If you work systematically, your weekly clean won't take more than an hour. Start by getting your gear together. You'll need your bucket, shovel, a trowel or scraper, a stiff brush, rubber gloves, and a mask. Remove the perches, nesting boxes, and the droppings board. Set the bedding from the nesting boxes aside, ready to reuse on the floor, and shovel the dirty bedding from the floor into your bucket. Scrape off the droppings, and sweep up the rest. While you're at it, keep an eye out for grey dust piles that look like cigarette ash. This is a sign of a red mite infestation, and you need to do something about it, we'll talk about what you need to do, later.

Once the coop is clean, take a few minutes to check for any potential problems like loose boards or evidence of leaks. When you're satisfied, add fresh bedding to the nesting boxes and the floor, and replace the perches and droppings board. If you want to sprinkle diatomaceous earth or mite powder, this is the time. If you have the time and the weather is good, leave the coop to air out for a few hours before you add fresh bedding. Put the old bedding and droppings into the compost heap, clean up your equipment, and wash your hands. It only takes a few minutes, and it'll make your life easier next week.

The deep bedding method is an alternative to cleaning out the bedding weekly. This system simply involves adding fresh bedding on top of the old bedding, then cleaning it out thoroughly a few times a year. The bedding composts in place and the heat it generates helps to keep the coop warm. If you choose to do it this way, when you scrape the droppings off the roosting bars and nesting boxes, sprinkle them on top of the old bedding before you add the fresh stuff.

If your chickens also have a static run, you need to add the cleaning of this to your weekly task list to prevent the run from harboring worms and disease. Fortunately, this is easier than cleaning the coop and only takes a few minutes. When the weather is dry, you can simply rake up the droppings and sprinkle poultry disinfectant or ground sanitizer to keep pests away and kill worm eggs. Covering the run with something like sand or hardwood chips will make cleaning easier.

At least twice a year, your coop will need a deep clean. Pick a nice, dry day and start first thing in the morning. This gives everything a good chance to dry thoroughly before you move the chickens back in. Start a deep clean by dismantling your coop as much as possible, then continue as you would for your weekly clean: remove the bedding and scrape up the droppings. Once all of the dry material is gone, thoroughly hose the coop down, soaking everything. If you have a pressure blaster, this is its chance to shine!

Once everything is wet, spray it all down with your preferred cleaning chemical, then thoroughly scrub it out with a stiff brush. If any parts are especially dirty, soak them in undiluted vinegar. Make sure you attend to every nook and cranny of the coop. If you've used vinegar, leave the coop open to air-dry for a while. If you've chosen to use a harsher chemical like bleach, rinse it off before leaving it to dry.

Most common maintenance tasks are either preventable through good routines (like airing the coop to prevent rot) or are straightforward to fix if you catch them early, like loose chicken wire, minor leaks, or sagging hinges. The longer you leave maintenance problems, the worse they'll get, and the longer it will take to fix them.

Wing, Claw and Beak Clipping

While chickens manage most of their grooming themselves, there are a few tasks that will fall to you: wing, claw and beak clipping. Chickens can't fly well, but a determined chicken can fly well enough to get over a low fence. The world-record holder managed to fly 301.5 ft in thirteen seconds! While your chickens probably won't get that far, clipping their wings will keep them closer to home. If your chickens don't even attempt to fly, then there's no need to clip their wings.

Wing-clipping cuts the ends off the primary flight feathers. You only need to clip the primary flight feathers on one wing, as that unbalances the chicken enough to stop it from flying. Done right, it's completely painless and similar to cutting hair. If you imagine that your arm is a wing, the flight cover feathers would be all along your arm. The primary flight feathers would be sticking out from your forearm, and the secondary flight feathers from your upper arm. Most chickens have ten primary flight feathers.

The key to successful wing-clipping is to avoid cutting feathers which are growing, as they still have a blood supply. You can identify these by looking under the wing at the shaft of the feather. The shaft of a growing feather looks dark rather than white. Do not cut these feathers, as there's a chance your chicken will bleed to death. The idea is to trim the primary flight feathers about halfway from the flight coverts. If the chicken can still fly, you might need to trim the secondary flight feathers too, but this is unusual.

To do this, you'll need:

- a helper (not absolutely necessary, but it makes the job much easier);

- a clean, sharp pair of scissors or a pair of nail clippers; and
- styptic powder, cornflour/cornstarch, or a bar of soap (just in case you need to control bleeding).

Sit down and lay the chicken on its back. Get your helper to hold the chicken while you stretch out the wing, check for growing feathers, and identify which feathers to cut. Once you know which feathers to cut, start cutting, working away from the chicken's body, towards the wingtip. If you cut a growing feather, control the bleeding by holding a pinch of styptic powder or cornflour against the tip of the feather, or push the tip of the bleeding feather into a bar of soap. When you're done, clean your scissors or nail clippers so they're ready for next time.

If you keep your chickens outside, the scratching and pecking will typically keep their beak and claws short enough to not cause a problem. From time to time, this simply isn't enough, and you'll need to trim a chicken's beak and claws; as if they become too long, a chicken can't scratch and peck properly. Let's be completely clear: I'm not talking about de-beaking. Cutting a chicken's beak so short that the bird can't use it is cruel and also illegal in most western countries.

If a chicken's claws are curling around towards the foot, you'll need to trim them. The process is very similar to clipping wings, and you need the same equipment. In this case, sturdy nail clippers work better than scissors. Hold the chicken on its back on your lap until it calms down. Wrapping it in a towel or asking someone to help you can make this easier the first time. Wipe the claws clean, so that you can see what you're doing. The quick is a small vein that supplies blood to the growing claw. As with wing clipping, avoid cutting the blood vessel. For chickens with light-colored claws, you can shine a bright light through the claw to find out where the quick stops. Aim to cut a short distance away from the end of the quick. Once you know where to cut, hold the toe, then use your nail clippers to clip the claw. If you can't see the quick, clip 1/16 of an inch off the claw at a time and keep checking the color. As you get closer to the quick, the claw gets darker. Very long claws have very long veins, so it will take several attempts over a few weeks to trim these back safely.

The only time a chicken's beak needs trimming is if the top beak is curling over the bottom, preventing them from eating properly. As well as the equipment you've used for clipping wings and claws, you'll also need a nail file and a damp tissue or cloth.

Wrap the chicken in a towel, hold it on its back, just as you did for claw and wing clipping, and inspect the beak. The area of the beak with a blood supply will look darker than the rest of the beak. Again, you need to avoid the dark area. If the beak is only a little bit too long, you can file it back with the nail file. File in one direction, away from the chicken's face, until the top beak just overhangs the lower beak. If it's too long to file down, trim it back with the clippers until it just overhangs the lower part of the beak, then use the nail file to smooth out the edges. When you're done, double-check that there are no rough spots left on the beak, then wipe the dust off with a damp tissue before you release your chicken.

Worming Chickens

There are two schools of thought among backyard chicken owners. The first group regularly worms their chickens or feeds them medicated feed to prevent worms; the second group tries to avoid worms through good hygiene and other natural methods, then treats any chickens who manage to get worms. Whichever group you fall into, preventing worms is a matter of good hygiene. Still, good hygiene won't prevent every case of worms.

If you want to worm your flock regularly, just in case, you'll need to find specific medications for different types of worms. If you're happy to use medication, you have two options: administer a dedicated preventative every three or six months, or buy medicated feed. The main concerns with using preventative medication are first: that the worms may become resistant to it, and therefore will be more challenging to treat; and second: that the treatment will be present in the eggs and meat that the chickens produce. The obvious advantage is that it's easy.

Some natural options for preventing worms include adding apple cider vinegar to your birds' water (one tablespoon per gallon) and commercially available herbal worming treatments that you can add to their feed or water. Whichever option you choose, you should follow the instructions on the box.

In the following section, I'll discuss how to butcher and store your chicken meat – should you choose to do so!

Butchering Chickens

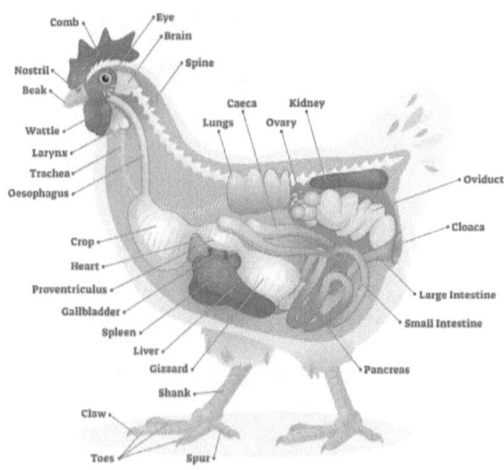

If you are keeping chickens for meat, the time will come where you'll need to butcher them. Here we'll cover how to decide when, and how, to kill them, and what to do once they're dead. While you can slaughter your meat chickens whenever you like, there are trade-offs. The longer you wait, the more you spend on feeding them, but if you kill them too early, they'll be too small. If you wait too long, some breeds are prone to health problems, and the meat can become tough. It depends on the breed, but I think the sensible time to slaughter a chicken is when it's stopped growing quickly. Most meat breeds will grow quickly for about eighteen to twenty weeks, then slow down, while some commercial meat breeds are fully grown at six weeks.

There are several ways to kill a chicken humanely, but by far the simplest is to either behead it or cut its throat. I strongly recommend buying a killing cone (a big metal funnel) to simplify the process.

If you'd like to see the butchering process visually, be sure to watch some tutorials on youtube.

Before you start, set up your working area. You'll need:

| At least two very sharp knives | A pinning knife (optional, but it helps with | A killing cone (also optional, but it makes the job easier) | Some way to hang the carcass by the feet (a hook |

	plucking)		and bungee cord work well)
Several buckets for blood, offcuts, and water	Water (a garden hose is ideal)	Gloves (optional, but they do make life easier)	Old clothes. You're definitely going to get dirty
A stable table, or another working surface. If it's difficult to clean, cover it with a large cloth	A large pot of hot water. You can use a stockpot, a large metal bucket on a gas burner, or anything else big enough for a chicken that will keep water hot	A thermometer	A cooler full of icy water
Paper towels	A cutting board	Zip-lock bags or heat-shrink bags big enough for	

		chickens	

Set up your workspace in a sensible sequence, and make sure your pot of water is hot (130-140F) before you start. You'll start at the killing cone, which you should attach to something about a foot above the bucket. You'll move from there to the hot water, then hang the chicken while you pluck it. After plucking, you'll go to your stable surface with a cutting board to remove entrails and other unnecessary parts, then drop the carcass in ice water. Pick your chicken (or chickens) the day before you plan to slaughter them, and don't feed them the night before. If their crop is empty, it's one less thing to worry about when you're butchering them.

When you're all set up and ready to go, catch a chicken. Hold it upside down until it stops struggling, then put it in the cone, so the head sticks out of the bottom. If you don't have a cone, hang the bird upside down by the legs. Take your very sharp knife, hold the head, and quickly cut the neck at the side of the jaw to sever the jugular. Hold the head to one side as the blood drains into the bucket. If you're not using a cone, the chicken might flap and twitch. This is a reflex, not a sign of distress.

When the chicken stops moving, cut the head off (you can leave this until later if you want), wash any dirt off the carcass, then dunk the carcass into the hot water for three or four minutes. You can either hold it by the feet or use a hook or tongs. If you're planning to use the feet, make sure you scald them too. Every few minutes, lift it slightly out of the water and tug a few feathers. When the feathers come out easily, it's ready to pluck.

To pluck the chicken, just grab the feathers and pull them out. I find plucking easier when I wear rubber gloves. Once you've got rid of the big feathers, rubber gloves help to get a grip on the smaller feathers. Some people find it easier to hang the chicken upside down while they do this, while others prefer to hold it. Experiment and see what works best for you. The large feathers leave "pins" behind. You can remove these with a pinning knife, which is similar to a butter knife. Scrape the pinning knife gently along the skin to remove the pins. If you want to use the feet, pull the skin off. Once you're done, hose it down to remove any feather remains before moving on to the next stage: gutting and cleaning the carcass.

While you're butchering, keep two buckets nearby for scraps: one for useful scraps, one for the rest.

Start by cutting off the legs at the joint. If you cut right in the V of the joint, you can avoid cutting the bone and blunting your knife. Drop the feet in the "useful scraps" bucket. If you haven't already removed the head, do it now, then cut the muscle around the neck, then break the spine and remove the remains of the neck. The neck goes in the "useful scraps" bucket, and the head goes in with the rest of the scraps.

The preen gland comes next. Lie the carcass on its stomach. The preen gland is the big lump at the tail end. Slice down behind it, through the spine, and scoop it out with the tip of your knife. Slide the knife along the spine to remove any remaining yellow tissue. Try not to puncture it or leave anything behind, or it will spoil the taste of the meat.

After removing the preen gland, roll the carcass over and slice the skin of the neck above the breastbone. Stick a finger into the slit, and tear down until you find the crop, esophagus, and windpipe. Working carefully, pull the esophagus and windpipe out of the neck and either break or cut the connecting tissue around the crop. If you rupture the crop, wash off the partially-digested feed before going any further.

Turn the carcass around so you can access the vent. Cut from about an inch above the vent to the base of the breastbone, but don't cut too deep: you don't want to break the intestines. If you do manage to puncture the intestines, rinse it off with bleach solution before continuing. Reach inside and run your hand around the ribs to ensure the intestines and other internal organs are free, then cut around the vent and gently pull it away from the body. The intestines will follow. Be careful not to break them! Once they're out, reach into the cavity for the lungs, windpipe, and anything else that's left inside.

Drop the bird into the iced water cooler to chill for at least thirty minutes - although a day is better. Once it's thoroughly cooled, remove it, pat it dry, and put it in either a zip lock bag or a heat-shrink bag in the fridge. I like to label the bag with the date - it helps keep track of which meat I need to use first.

While it's chilling, sort out the giblets (i.e., the pile of innards). You should have intestines, lungs, heart, liver, kidneys, and gizzard. You can start by separating the intestines and dropping them in the "useless scraps" bucket. The heart, lungs, and kidneys can go straight into the "useful scraps" bucket, leaving you with the gizzard and the liver. If you want to save the gizzard, you'll need to clean it. Cut it open from hole to hole, empty the contents (grit and food), and rinse it. When it's clean, you'll see a yellow lining. You need to peel this away. Once you get started, the rest comes off easily. Once you're finished, put it with the other useful scraps.

The key to using the liver is to remove the gallbladder without contaminating the rest of the liver. The gallbladder is the green part that looks a bit like a pickle. Before you drop the liver in with the useful scraps, cut the gallbladder away, along with a little bit of the liver. It's not poisonous, but it will make your liver taste very bitter.

Leave the bagged birds in the fridge for a few days before eating or freezing. Otherwise, they'll be tough and tasteless. You should leave them for long enough to go through rigor mortis, then relax again. For smaller birds, this will be about thirty-six hours; for larger birds, two days. Once it's rested, you can either cook it or freeze it.

Chapter 12 - Making Money & Showing Off

If you want to sell products from your chickens, eggs are the obvious place to start. Before you start selling any animal products (like eggs) for human consumption, you need to research your local laws. In the UK, you don't need to clean your eggs unless they are dirty, and you don't need to refrigerate them; in the USA, you have to clean and refrigerate them. Both sets of rules are intended to prevent salmonella. The easy way to sidestep the debate is to keep your nesting boxes clean and to not leave the eggs in the nesting boxes long enough to get dirty.

If you intend to sell your eggs commercially, you'll need to grade them in accordance with the local laws, but most countries have an exemption for farm-gate sales. While it may be tempting to reuse old egg cartons, resist that temptation; if you use branded cartons, you may get in trouble with the company. Either buy new cartons from your local farm store (they're not expensive) or ask your customers to bring their own cartons. Don't forget to mark the eggs (and cartons, if you're providing them) with a "Best Before" date along with your name and address. That way, when they run out, they can remember where to come back to for more.

If you have a rooster, you don't aren't limited to selling eggs for eating: there's a growing demand for fertilized eggs. If you have purebred or heritage breeds, this market can be quite lucrative; some people are willing to pay more than $5 per egg, but you'll need to be very careful to select high-quality chickens to start with.

If you decide to sell fertilized eggs online, consider buying some from an assortment of other breeders. Find out what works for shipping and packaging, and, more importantly, what doesn't, before you start trying to ship eggs anywhere.

After eggs, the next obvious products to sell are chickens. When you sell live animals, as well as being familiar with the law, you need to know where you stand with regard to your personal ethics. If someone wants to buy one chick for their child at Easter, will you sell it to them if you don't think they can look after it? If you're selling live meat birds, will you check that the buyer knows how to slaughter them humanely? Or is that beyond the scope of your responsibilities? I'm not going to try to answer those questions for you, but it's worth thinking them through for yourself.

Especially around Easter, day-old chicks are a popular purchase, but some people also buy chicks to top up their flocks in autumn. Even if you have a broody hen to hatch your eggs, it's easier to plan ahead of time if you hatch them with an incubator. Chicks are worth a few dollars each for common breeds and straight run (unsexed); but more if they're sexed or heritage breeds. If you choose to sell sexed chicks, work out what to do with your leftover rooster chicks.

Another decision with regard to chicks is whether you'll stick to selling them locally, or if you'll ship to buyers elsewhere. If you want to ship, you'll need to work out the logistics, and in most countries, you'll need a permit or certificate to prove that the chicks are healthy. If you're willing to put in a bit more effort, consider selling pullets. You'll need to raise them, but by the time you sell them, you'll know their gender and the hens won't be too far from laying. This means buyers will pay more for the convenience of not having to raise the hen themselves. Again, the price per hen will vary depending on breed and location, but $15-$40 is the normal range.

Fresh, high-quality chicken meat is just as popular as fresh eggs, so if you're breeding meat birds, this is an obvious way to make money. The specific laws for slaughtering animals and selling meat from home vary depending on where you live. Before you start, make sure you comply with the laws in your area, or you could find yourself in hot water. If you can't abide by the laws, find out whether a local slaughterhouse will process your birds for you. If not, you could sell them alive for your customers to slaughter and butcher at home. If your chickens are free-range and raised on organic feed, don't forget to tell your customers: they'll be willing to pay more!

To breed chickens, you need one rooster for every ten hens. Since around half of all eggs are male, you'll definitely end up with more roosters than you need. You can sell them alive, sell them for meat (or as meat), or process them for personal use. If you have a heritage breed, selling your purebred roosters could be profitable, while selling them for meat is more practical for common breeds.

When your hens stop laying, what will you do with them? If they're family pets, it could make sense to keep them; if they're not, you could sell them for stew. Older hens can be quite tough, particularly if they've been active foragers, but a crockpot solves that, and they taste just as good. If you sell your old hens for $3-$5, they're a bargain for the customers, and they won't be a constant drain on your feed budget. If you have a steady supply of laying hens, you could sell them while they're still laying. You'll make more money from the sale of a laying hen than a stewing one!

For heritage breeds or show birds, poultry auctions are a great place to get rid of many surplus birds in a hurry, but you won't make as much as you would selling them one at a time. Eggs and meat aren't chickens' only marketable products: feathers and manure are also abundant.

Crafters use chicken feathers in everything from jewelry and home decor to fly fishing lures. Especially if you have chickens with fancy feathers, it's worth saving feathers during molting season. If you're into crafting, you can use them in your crafts and sell the products; otherwise, sell the feathers directly on popular sites like Etsy or eBay.

Chicken manure is an unavoidable by-product of raising chickens. You have to clean it up regularly, so you may as well bag it and sell it to local gardeners. It's high in nitrogen, and after a few weeks, it'll be a valuable addition to their (or your) soil.

The longer you keep chickens, the more you'll learn about the perfect equipment or the perfect feed. If you design the perfect homemade feed, a feeder that fixes a common problem, or a fantastic new coop design for your flock, market it. If it works for you, it'll probably work for other people in the same situation, so start a small business and sell it!

Keeping chickens is a journey of constant discovery. If writing's your thing, look for ways to monetize it. Start a blog, write a book about caring for your favorite breed, or offer to talk to your local schools about chickens.

Making money isn't always just about selling things: renting works as well. Kids love watching chickens hatch, but schools and science centers might not want to buy an incubator. Offer to rent yours out when you're not using it. The same applies to your chickens. See if anyone wants to rent chickens as pest control in their garden, as set-dressing for a theatre, or as part of a demonstration for schoolchildren. You never know until you ask!

Best Breeds for Showing:

Show breeds are picked for their eye-catching colors and fancy feathers. The key considerations are body-type, color, and feather pattern. Tastes vary, so if you're interested in getting into shows and competitions, spend some time working out what you find attractive, what breeds are accepted at the shows you're interested in, and what's popular in your region. Once you've narrowed your options, consider how much work is required to look after each of your preferred breeds and prepare them for shows, then balance that with how much work you're willing to put in. Talking to breeders at shows is a great way to learn; everyone loves talking about their passion, and experienced chicken breeders are no exception.

Some popular show breeds that aren't too difficult for beginners are:

All sorts of bantams - I covered Bantams earlier, but they make perfect show birds because, among other things, they're small. This makes them easier to handle and transport, and they're cute. This is a definite bonus when traveling to and from shows.

Orpingtons - In a similar vein, Orpingtons are also popular show chickens. They're good looking, sociable and easy to handle.

Faverolles - Faverolles are quite rare. They're often called "the French poodle of chicken breeds." They have five toes on each foot and come in white and salmon with delicately laced feathering all over their bodies. They're gentle

chickens that are easy to handle but are often bullied by other breeds in mixed flocks.

Brahmas - Brahmas grow to ten pounds or more, and have dark, light or buff feathers down to their feet. They're gentle and easy to handle, which makes them a suitable choice as show birds.

Houdans - Houdans are an old French breed that, apart from the mottled Houdan, which is black with white splashes, are either all-black or all-white colored. They're gentle,  calm, and friendly, with a big, fluffy topknot. This makes them popular show birds, but also targets of bullies in mixed flocks. If you keep Houdans, you'll need to trim their topknots regularly; otherwise they won't be able to see!

Raising chickens for exhibitions and shows requires a lot of work and a lot of money, but it can be incredibly satisfying. The key to success in shows and exhibitions is picking the right bird. To do that, you need to become intimately familiar with the standards for your chosen breed.

In general, shows don't allow hybrid or mixed breed birds; you'll need a purebreed, and it's safest to buy chicks from professional breeders. Brace yourself for when you ask for the price: purebred heritage chicks can be $50 or $60 each. Especially when you're getting started, don't over-extend yourself. Start with one or two breeds, then work up from there. When you're choosing a bird for exhibition, your primary concern should be finding the best specimen of that breed; however, other factors area also important.

You need a breed that suits your available space, your local climate, and for whatever other use you might plan for the birds. If you primarily keep chickens for eggs, it makes sense to pick a show breed that's also a good layer. At shows, chickens that are calm and don't mind being handled have a great advantage over highly-strung, nervous birds. If you don't keep them isolated, aggressive chickens are likely to end up with injuries or damaged feathers before a show, which won't help you at all. Many people prefer bantams or small breeds as show birds, purely because they're easier to handle and transport than larger breeds.

Once you have your chick, you'll need to raise it. While the basic concepts are the same for all chickens, show chickens have a few extra principles that you'll need to consider.

First, don't let your purebreeds mix until you're sure that there's no rooster around. Purebred lines don't stay pure if they breed with other breeds, as you might guess. Next, as much as chickens enjoy it, letting show chickens free-range is asking for trouble.

All you need is for your prime show hen to cut herself on a sharp rock, get her feathers caught in a fence, or hurt her leg in a mole hole. You can't exhibit a bird that doesn't look perfect. In a similar vein, don't let show birds socialize with too many other chickens. Bullying or pecking order disputes can cause injuries (at worst) or make the bird skittish (at best). To prevent them from getting lonely, keep them in groups of two or three in a separate pen.

Do you remember how I said you need to become intimately familiar with the standards for your chosen breed? Well, as show season approaches, you'll need to really start applying that knowledge. Take a good look at your chickens and choose the one that's closest to the breed's "Standards of Perfection." That will be your show bird (or birds). The earlier you identify any deviations from perfection, the earlier you can cull those birds from your flock. You can keep the imperfect birds as pets, laying hens or meat birds, sell them for the same reasons, or kill them. Whatever you do, don't keep imperfect birds within your show flock.

Well before the show, contact the show superintendent, find out what paperwork you'll need, and collect it in a folder. At least eight weeks before the show, check your birds carefully for broken or missing feathers, parasites, overly-long claws/beak, or other aesthetic defects. If you remove broken feathers at this stage, they'll have time to grow back before the show. To remove a broken feather safely and painlessly, don't just pull it out. Cut it off above the vein (if it's still growing), then split the remainder along its length. A few days later, you'll be able to pull it out easily.

In the weeks leading up to a show, handle your show birds often, play the radio near their cages, move them between cages, and walk past them to get them used to what they'll encounter during the show. As show day approaches, start preparing. A week beforehand, trim the birds' wings and claws if necessary. At least three or four days before the show, you'll need to prepare your chickens properly. Wash them, dry them, give them a pedicure, then isolate them somewhere they can't get themselves into trouble.

To bathe your chicken, you'll need a bucket or plastic tub big enough for the chicken, and a smaller tub, bucket, shower or hose to pour or spray warm water. Fill the tub with warm water that's shallow enough for the chicken to stand up comfortably, place them in, and give them time to settle down. When they've calmed down, use your smaller tub or hose to completely soak them. Wash them a few times with dog or baby shampoo, rinsing them off in between. When you're done, give them a final rinse and make sure there's no shampoo left before you towel dry them.

Once they're towel-dried, you can moisturize their comb, wattle, and earlobes with something like hand cream, cocoa butter, coconut oil, or Vaseline, then blow-dry them. Some chickens enjoy being blow-dried, some hate it. Either way, make sure you don't burn them: keep the dryer on warm, not hot, and don't get too close.

If your chicken has extra feathers on their face, you can pluck them with a pair of tweezers before you clean their face, comb, and legs with a few cotton-tips dipped in warm water, or a toothbrush (for stubborn dirt). While you're doing that, check their beak and claws. If needed, give them a last going-over with a file, then put your chicken in a clean cage with fresh bedding while they dry off.

At your first show, wear clothes you're willing to get dirty, arrive early, and focus on watching, learning, meeting people, and asking questions. Don't forget to bring your folder of paperwork along. Stick with feeding your show chickens only scratch and grit on the day; this helps to keep the droppings solid, which makes it easier to keep the chickens clean during the show. Don't feed them until after judging.

When you arrive, start by finding out where you and your chickens are supposed to be and what time they'll be judged, then get them settled in. If you want to, you can do some last-minute primping to make sure they look their best. It's a good idea to lock their cages with small padlocks, just to prevent any misunderstandings. During the day, take notes and photos, talk to the other exhibitors and the judges, and find out what they're looking for and how things work. Throughout the day, and at least half an hour before judging, make sure your chicken is clean, and that all droppings are removed from the cage.

At some shows, you may have a conversation with the judge after the contest. The judges are experts, so take advantage of this to get some tips. Just before closing, it's a perfect time to visit the sales area. Vendors often offer discounts to avoid taking their stock home. When you get home, focus on safety. You and your chickens could be carrying pathogens or parasites, so immediately isolate your show chickens, disinfect your boots, wash your clothes, and take a shower before you visit the rest of your flock. It's sensible to give them a going-over with flea powder or spray, just in case. If you've bought new chickens at the show, they'll need to go into quarantine to protect your main flock (refer back to Chapter 7 if you need to).

Conclusion

Well, congratulations on making it through! If you've made it this far, you've learned absolutely everything you need to get started keeping backyard chickens. But please don't forget: knowledge is worthless unless you go out there and put it into action!

By now, you've learned about the characteristics of different breeds of chicken and how to pick the right breed for you. You've calculated how many chickens will fit in your garden (or even your house!), and what sort of housing and fencing will be most effective in keeping them safe. Given that you've put in the time to learn, I hope you've progressed (or are planning to progress) to buying or making housing for your chickens, selecting, buying or hatching some chickens, and caring for them.

The excitement of collecting your first egg, or watching your first chick hatch is something you – and maybe your children - will never forget. Chickens and humans have lived together for at least eight thousand years. Keeping backyard chickens isn't just a way to continue that relationship; it's also a ticket into a wonderful and supportive community of others who love their chickens. Amazing and long-standing friendships have started with a simple conversation at a chicken show, or even with a neighbor or stranger who's just curious about chickens. While people traditionally keep chickens for practical reasons, chickens aren't just another food source or simply for show. The more time you spend with them, the more you'll realize that each chicken is a beautiful individual in its own right. You start by raising them for eggs or meat, but don't be surprised if you find yourself breeding and showing rare chickens ten years down the line.

Backyard chickens are like a gateway drug to other sustainable lifestyle choices, from a simple vegetable garden to full-blown backyard homesteading or even animal-rights activism. It's good for your health, good for your garden, good for your community, and good for the environment. The more I learn, the more I realize I still have to learn, and my chickens are my best teachers. I hope this is the beginning of a long, satisfying and fruitful journey for you and your new chickens. *If you have enjoyed reading this book, then you'll love my latest book "[Worm Bins - The Experts' Guide To Upcycling Your Food Scraps & Revitalising Your Garden](#)". It shows you why Worms, incredibly, are more ecologically important than Pandas, and teaches you how to set up your first worm bin & become an expert vermiculturist! To turn your household waste into highly fertile black-gold-dust, click the link above to get the book and learn how it's done.*

Don't forget to help other aspiring chicken-keepers find this book by leaving a **positive (hopefully 5*) review on Amazon.** Thank you so much for reading, and best of luck in your new hobby!

Best wishes,
Geoff Evans

P.S. You can find the most frequently asked chicken keeping questions below…

Commonly Asked Questions (& Answers)

Terminology

What's the difference between a hen and a rooster?
A hen is female, and a rooster is male.

What's the difference between a cockerel and a pullet?
A cockerel is a young rooster, while a pullet is a young hen.

What's a broody hen?
A broody hen keeps trying to hatch eggs. She sits on them all day and night, except when she has to eat, drink, and poop.

What's a bantam?
A bantam is a small chicken, about a quarter to half the size of a regular chicken.

What's molting?
Every year, usually in autumn, chickens' feathers fall out and regrow. They often stop laying while they're molting.

What's the deep litter method?
It's a method for managing coop bedding. Instead of cleaning it out daily, you just leave it where it is and put another layer of fresh bedding on top. The bedding starts to compost in the coop, and you clean it out every four to six months.

What's scratch?
Scratch is a name for grains, including corn and wheat, that you can feed chickens as a treat.

What are straight run chicks?
Straight run chicks are a mixture of male and female chicks.

Buying Chickens

Should I buy straight run chicks?

Straight run chicks are cheaper. If you only want hens, you should avoid straight run chicks unless you have something useful to do with the roosters.

What is the best egg-laying breed (layer)?

There are lots, but Rhode Island red, leghorn, golden comet, Plymouth rock, and Ameraucana are very popular (see Chapter 2).

What is the best meat breed (broiler)?

Cornish cross, Jersey giant, La Bresse, Delaware, and freedom ranger are popular meat breeds (see Chapter 2).

Looking After Chickens

What should I feed my chickens?
Choose an appropriate commercial feed for their age. Usually, starter pellets or mash until they're about eight weeks old, grower pellets until they're about eighteen weeks old, then layer/combination starter-grower pellets until they're eighteen weeks old, then pure layer ration (see Chapter 5).

Can I feed my chickens treats?
Absolutely! But not too many. Kitchen scraps, scratch (grain), and vegetables are great treats for chickens (see Chapter 5).

How do chickens mate?
The rooster climbs on the hen's back, holds her by the head or the back of the neck with his beak, and uses his feet to stabilize himself while he inserts his papilla into the hen's vent (see Chapter 6).

Do I need to separate my rooster chicks when they grow up?
No. If they grow up together, they'll generally get along.

Will my hens lay eggs if I don't have a rooster?
Yes, but the eggs won't be fertile (see Chapter 6).

How many roosters do I need?
If you're breeding them, one rooster for about ten hens is a good ratio. If you're not breeding them, you don't need a rooster.

How can I tell if a chick's a rooster?
Even if you're an expert, it's difficult to identify the sex of a chick until they grow up a bit (see Chapter 4).

Why do roosters crow?
I have no idea! Some people say he's announcing his territory or reminding the hens he's there. He could be challenging another rooster. He could be just enjoying the sound of his own voice - but don't we all? Only he knows for sure.

Why aren't my chickens laying?
Winter, stress, age, molting, and sickness are the main possibilities (see Chapter 6).

My hens' eggs have thin or soft shells. What should I do?
Feed them oyster shells as a calcium supplement.

My hens are eating their eggs. What should I do?
Feed them oyster shells as a calcium supplement. If that doesn't work, check the section earlier in this chapter about dealing with egg-eating.

How do I introduce my new chickens to my existing flock?
Slowly, over a few weeks (see Chapter 7).

How long do chickens usually live?
Usually, seven or eight years if you look after them properly (see Chapter 1).

What should I do about predators?
Identify them, then work out the best way to handle that specific predator (see Chapter 8).

Will my cat and dog get on with my chickens?
It depends. Wait until the chickens have settled in properly before you introduce them to your pets, and be ready to step in if there's a problem.

Will my children get on with my chickens?
The chickens probably won't be too concerned as long as the children are well-behaved. Make sure your children know how to interact with chickens before you introduce them.

Do chickens attract pests?
Not if you clean up and secure the feed.

What should I feed my chickens?
Appropriate commercial feed for their age and type. See Chapter 5.

Do I need a heat lamp?
Not unless you live in a very cold climate or you're raising chicks. If the coop isn't too big, chickens can usually keep warm by fluffing up their feathers and huddling together.

How tall do my fences need to be?
Six feet is standard. Some chickens could fly over that, but not many. You can also use aviary netting over the fences to keep the chickens in and protect them from aerial predators.

What sort of bedding should I use?
Pine shavings, straw, or sand (see Chapter 3).

How much space do I need in the coop and run?
About three square feet per bird in the coop, and at least ten square feet per bird in the run. (see Chapter 3).

Is it safe to paint the inside of my coop?

Yes, as long as you use non-toxic paint and make sure it's dry and ventilated before you let the chickens in.

What should I use for perches?
Flat untreated 4 x 2 inch wood, or large smooth branches (see Chapter 3).

How much roosting space do I need?
At least eight inches per chicken (see Chapter 3).

How high should the roosting perches be?
About eighteen to twenty-four inches above the floor.

How many nesting boxes do I need, and how big should they be?
One per three or four hens. They should be about a cubic foot (see Chapter 3).

How do I keep my waterers from freezing?
Buy heated waterers, or put a heat lamp above the waterer.

How many eggs will my hens lay?

Somewhere between 50 and 280 eggs per year, depending on the breed (see Chapter 2).

Do I have to wash the eggs?
Only if they're dirty (see Chapter 6).

When will my hens start laying eggs?
Usually, about eighteen to twenty weeks, but it depends on the breed and the season (see Chapter 2).

How long do hens lay eggs?
It depends on the breed, but usually about two or three years.

Should I worry if one of my hens lays an egg without a shell?
Don't worry, but do start feeding all your hens oyster shell as a calcium supplement.

How long does an egg take to hatch?
Usually, twenty-one days, but some bantam breeds lay eggs that hatch about day eighteen or nineteen (see Chapter 6).

Can I eat fertilized eggs?
Yep.

If there's a red spot in my egg, is it safe to eat?
Yes, it's just a blood spot. It's normal and perfectly safe to eat.

Do I have to clip my chickens' claws?
Only if they're curling around or making it difficult for the chickens to walk (see Chapter 11).

Do I have to clip my chickens' wings?
Only if the chickens keep trying to fly and escape (see Chapter 11).

One of my hens has something pink sticking out of her vent. Is that a problem?
Yes, it's probably a prolapsed vent (see Chapter 9).

It's cold, and my chicken's comb has turned purple or black. What's wrong?
It's probably frostbite (see Chapter 9).

Is bird flu a problem in backyard chickens?
Not normally (see Chapter 9).

I think one of my hens is sick. What do I do?
First, isolate her from the flock and check whether any other chickens are sick. Then consult a vet (see Chapter 9).

Why are my chicken's feathers falling out?
They could be molting, sick, or stressed (see Chapter 9).

References

Mitchell, A. D., Conway, J. M., & Potts, W. J. (1996). Body composition analysis of pigs by dual-energy x-ray absorptiometry. *Journal of Animal Science*, 74(11), 2663.
https://doi.org/10.2527/1996.74112663x

Images attained via Freepik.com Premium Subscription:
Subscription ID available on request -
Image Authors: @lifeonwhite, @cynoclub, @user2885513, @ingram, @lunamarina, @ziaurasouthwest, @ambhermann, @sylv1rob1, @pumppump, @brgfx, @normaals, @freepik, @ksyusha_yanovich

Buy Geoff's 'Worm Bins' Book:
(Amazon)
[CLICK HERE]()

www.ingramcontent.com/pod-product-compliance
Lightning Source LLC
Chambersburg PA
CBHW021432080526
44588CB00009B/508